DISCOVERING GOLDEN GATE PARK

A LOCAL'S GUIDE

Marta Lindsey

with Nancy Botkin

MOUNTAINEERS BOOKS

To my best-ever companions in the best-ever park:
Drew, Helena, and Elise

MOUNTAINEERS BOOKS is dedicated to the exploration, preservation, and enjoyment of outdoor and wilderness areas.

1001 SW Klickitat Way, Suite 201, Seattle, WA 98134
800-553-4453, www.mountaineersbooks.org

Printed in China
First edition, 2026

Design and layout: Melissa McFeeters
Cartographer: Pease Press
All photographs by the author unless credited otherwise
Cover photographs: front, clockwise from top left: *pagoda in the Japanese Tea Garden, Monterey cypress at the Botanical Garden, Conservatory of Flowers, Dutch Windmill, Huntington Falls* (Photos by Jim Watkins, except Conservatory, by Marta Lindsey); spine: *California golden poppies*; back cover, *Heroes Grove, great blue herons* (Photo by Robert Ho)
Frontispiece: *The park has four off-leash areas, plus dogs are allowed almost everywhere on leash.*
Leave No Trace Seven Principles © Leave No Trace, www.LNT.org

Library of Congress Cataloging-in-Publication data is on file for this title at https://lccn.loc.gov/2025026979. An ebook record is available at https://lccn.loc.gov/2025026980.

Mountaineers Books titles may be purchased for corporate, educational, or other promotional sales, and our authors are available for a wide range of events. For information on special discounts or booking an author, contact our customer service at 800-553-4453 or mbooks@mountaineersbooks.org.

Printed on FSC®-certified materials

FSC www.fsc.org MIX Paper | Supporting responsible forestry FSC® C188448

ISBN (paperback): 978-1-68051-734-7
ISBN (ebook): 978-1-68051-735-4

An independent nonprofit publisher since 1960

Contents

THE WILD SIDE: FINDING NATURE IN THE PARK 133

WALKS AND HIKES 157

Land Acknowledgment

GOLDEN GATE PARK is located within the unceded ancestral homeland of the Ramaytush Ohlone, the original inhabitants of the San Francisco Peninsula.

This acknowledgment was provided by the Association of Ramaytush Ohlone. Learn more at ramaytush.org.

Overview of Golden Gate Park

MUSEUMS & ATTRACTIONS

1 Dutch Windmill
2 Beach Chalet
3 Murphy Windmill
4 Bison paddock
5 De Young Museum
6 Music Concourse
7 Bandshell
8 California Academy of Sciences
9 Sharon Art Studio
10 Kezar Stadium
11 McLaren Lodge

RECREATION & SPORTS

1 Beach Chalet Athletic Fields
2 Archery range
3 Golf course
4 Bercut Equitation Field
5 Pétanque court
6 Senior center
7 Casting pools
8 Model Yacht Club
9 Polo Field and Stadium
10 Parcourse
11 Disc golf course
12 Skatin' Place
13 Handball/racquetball courts
14 Big Rec Ball Field
15 Lawn bowling
16 Goldman Tennis Center
17 Horseshoe courts
18 Zion Skate Plaza
19 Kezar Pavilion
20 Bocce courts
21 Fitness area
22 Nate Thurmond Panhandle Basketball Courts

DOG FACILITIES

1 Dog training area (fenced)
2 Dog run at Sunset Boulevard and MLK Drive
3 Dog run at 5th Avenue and Lincoln
4 Dog run at Kezar Stadium

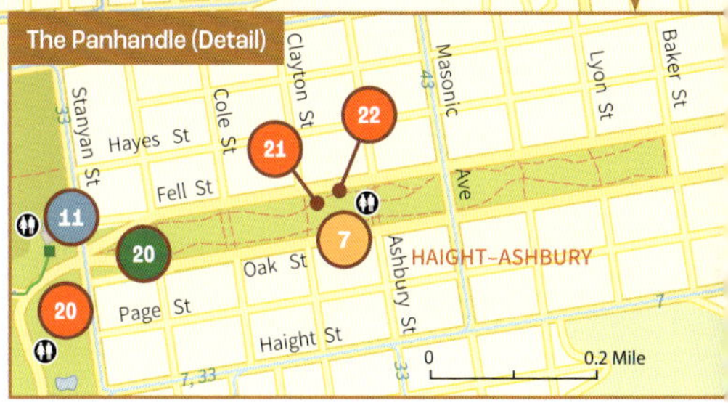

GARDENS & GROVES

1 Queen Wilhlemina Garden
2 Hellman Hollow
3 Marx Meadow
4 Redwood Memorial Grove
5 14th Avenue East Meadow
6 Rose Garden
7 Heroes Grove
8 Japanese Tea Garden
9 Shakespeare Garden
10 Botanical Garden
11 John McLaren Rhododenron Dell
12 National AIDS Memorial Grove
13 Conservatory of Flowers
14 Dahlia Dell
15 Breast Cancer Memorial Garden
16 Fuschia Dell
17 Peacock Meadow
18 Robin Williams Meadow
19 CommUNITY Garden
20 Sue Bierman Grove

PLAYGROUNDS

1 Playground at Beach Chalet Athletic Fields
2 Boat Playground
3 Mothers' Meadow Playground
4 Blue Playground
5 Carousel
6 Koret Children's Quarter
7 Panhandle Playground

SAN FRANCISCO'S CROWN JEWEL

AT ALMOST HALF THE LENGTH of San Francisco, with the Pacific Ocean running along its western edge, Golden Gate Park is arguably the best and most beautiful urban park anywhere. More than twenty-four million people visit this park every year from around the world—and just down the street (like me). In it, you will find the heart of San Francisco beating strongly, with creativity, community, and culture in every corner. You also can find true solitude and wildness within its 1,017 acres.

Golden Gate Park was born out of the Gold Rush and a growing population's realization that San Francisco would only be a great city if it had a great park. Transforming a lot of windswept sand dunes into forests, gardens, and lawns took guts, imagination, and some genius engineering by unsung hero William Hammond Hall. The legendary park superintendent and tree-lover John McLaren was crucial in carrying on Hall's work for more than half a century and locking in the vision parkgoers experience today: a green and welcoming respite from city living. But Golden Gate Park is so much more than the lawns, trees, benches, and sports fields you can find at any park. This park has many sides, intriguing stories, and hidden secrets, plus destinations and experiences you won't find anywhere else. Whether you're visiting Golden Gate Park for the first time or already know it well, I hope this guide will help you discover more than you ever expected.

Long Before the Park

Fifteen thousand years ago, the peninsula next to the Pacific Ocean now known as San Francisco wasn't a peninsula at all. It was part of a coastal plain, with a wide,

Opposite: The story of how Golden Gate Park became the park we know and love today may surprise you. *(Photo by Jim Watkins)*

deep river valley. Over time, the river carried and deposited large amounts of granite sand eroded from the mountains (now called the Sierra Nevada). Saber-toothed cats and woolly mammoths walked around what would someday become Golden Gate Park. But the last ice age was ending. The water that had been locked up in glaciers and ice sheets for a very long time was slowly melting, filling the floodplains and valley like a bathtub. Eventually, water surrounded a chunk of land on three sides, creating a peninsula.

The peninsula and nearby lands were home to Indigenous people known as the Ramaytush Ohlone. When Spanish colonists arrived in the late 1700s, a tribe within the Ramaytush Ohlone referred to today as the Yelamu, lived specifically in the area that's now San Francisco. Five Yelamu villages are documented as having been in San Francisco (all near the Bay), but little is known about their daily lives. We do know there would have been abundant wild strawberries and acorns, known to be part of the Yelamu people's diet, growing in what is now the park.

After the Gold Rush started in 1849, San Francisco's population quickly increased to 50,000 by the mid-1850s. As the city grew, so did the recognition that a large public park was needed. *(Photo courtesy of Greg Gaar)*

No members of the Yelamu Tribe survived years of being forced to live and work in the Spanish missions. However, today some living descendants of the Ramaytush Ohlone are reclaiming their cultural heritage and traditions, sharing and celebrating their art, history, and knowledge in a variety of ways.

A City Born Almost Overnight

After Spanish colonists arrived, and leading up to the start of the Mexican-American war in 1846, a small settlement was established in what began to be called "San Francisco" with fewer than a thousand individuals, including Mexican, American, European, and Indigenous people. Technically, the land was part of Mexico, which had successfully won independence from Spain in 1821.

When the United States and Mexico signed a treaty in 1848, California's lands were put into American hands. What timing! That's the year gold was first discovered in the state. The Gold Rush officially began in 1849, bringing droves of people seeking wealth and opportunity. California officially became a state the following year, and San Francisco a city within it. By the mid-1850s, San Francisco had around 50,000 people. This new port city and the first major city in California was on its way to greatness.

A Great City Needs a Great Park

By the mid-1860s, there were about 100,000 people living mostly in the northeastern corner of the city. City leaders wanted to turn the page on the city's rough-and-tumble beginnings and become more cosmopolitan. There was a growing sense that some kind of "pleasure grounds" would be good for everyone, and that to be a great city meant having a great park. Meanwhile, it was not going unnoticed that New York City had opened the first section of Central Park in 1858.

Park advocates were getting traction on the idea of a great park, but it then became a question of *where*. While some wanted to put the park on the undeveloped west side of the city, others thought this idea was pure folly. At the time, the west side was perceived as a distant wasteland. A map of San Francisco from 1853 labeled this part of the city as the "Great Sand Bank" because it was mostly just large, rolling hills of sand. The dunes (some reaching 100 feet tall) were impossible to traverse, even with horses, and the powerful winds off the Pacific that shaped the dunes would blast sand in the face of anyone who dared to visit.

Not only was the public increasingly questioning locating the park on the west side, but the two men who designed New York City's Central Park—Frederick Law Olmsted and Calvert Vaux—had a competing proposal. Their idea was for a 120-acre park in Hayes Valley (the neighborhood near the current City Hall) with a greenway connecting it to the San Francisco Bay and to Market Street. Olmsted had also thrown down the gauntlet in his opposition of the idea of a west side park. He thought it would be impossible to create the kind of park that people expected on the Great Sand Bank. "It would not be wise nor safe to undertake to form a park upon any plan which assumed as a certainty that trees which would delight the eye can be made to grow near San Francisco," wrote Olmsted.

But the price tag for land near downtown, local politics, and a small group of prominent citizens who wanted to go big with the park led back to the west side for the final location. It was then up to the newly formed Outside Lands Committee to then get it done. In 1868, the five members of the committee (who were all on the Board of Supervisors for the City of San Francisco) successfully negotiated with the handful of people who had "homesteaded" parts of the desired parkland (which mostly meant putting down piles of rocks to claim some land), to secure 1,014 acres for a park. Later on, the streets along the Panhandle were named for the committee members: Stanyan, Shrader, Cole, Clayton, and Ashbury.

On April 4, 1870, legislation was passed creating "what shall be known as Golden Gate Park." The legislation also created the "Avenue" we know today as the Panhandle, which is technically part of Golden Gate Park.

What happened next was crucial: a twenty-four-year-old civil engineer—largely self-taught—named William Hammond Hall submitted the lowest bid and won the job of surveying and mapping the parkland. Hall had been working as a surveyor, including for the US Army Corps of Engineers. He had also visited Central Park as well as parks in Paris and London.

Hall surveyed and laid out a design for the park that was remarkably like what we experience today in terms of character, layout, and topography. He had the wisdom to keep the hills to help block the wind and make the park more interesting. He sketched out winding roads instead of straight ones to prevent wind tunnels. Whether or not they threw around the word *genius* in the 1800s, all signs point to Hall having been one.

This 1910 photo of the undeveloped Sunset District shows what the dunes of the "Great Sand Bank" were like. The Murphy Windmill can be seen on the far right of the horizon. *(Photo by Willard Worden, courtesy of Greg Gaar)*

Hall was then made superintendent of the park and took on the seemingly impossible at a breakneck pace. On the far western end of the park, Hall had wooden walls built as the basis of a large artificial dune to block the wind coming off the Pacific Ocean and keep further sand dunes from forming. Through rapid trial and error, Hall figured out how to stabilize the dunes and turn sand into soil. By first soaking barley and native lupine seeds and then planting them together, the fast-growing barley protected the lupine from the wind as the lupine sent roots deep into the sand. This held the sand in place—and meant that other plants and trees could take root. Hall had already started a nursery in the park, which was growing hundreds of thousands of tree seedlings. He quickly found that drought-tolerant eucalyptus, Monterey pine, and Monterey cypress trees grew incredibly fast and could then serve as windbreaks, allowing other types of trees to grow.

Meanwhile, Hall was working at breakneck speed in the "Avenue" (known today as the Panhandle) and the far eastern end of the park. These areas would serve as a proof of concept for San Franciscans while the rest of the park could be dealt with over time. But astonishingly, within just five years, much of the park was taking shape. Seven hundred acres of dunes had been stabilized. The grassy meadows and forested glades that people wanted were being realized. Hall, who proved to be both a master engineer *and* master gardener, had cracked the code.

Olmsted happily ate his words in a letter to Hall, writing: "I cannot too strongly express my admiration of the spirit and method which characterizes your undertaking, and I do not doubt that it will be rewarded with results such as I have not hitherto thought it reasonable to expect under the circumstances." Indeed!

Central Park vs. Golden Gate Park

San Francisco and New York City have plenty of long-running rivalries. But which city has the superior "crown jewel" park? Really, there's no contest.

	Central Park	Golden Gate Park
ESTABLISHED	1858	1870
DESIGNED BY	Frederick Law Olmsted and Calvert Vaux	William Hammond Hall
VISITORS PER YEAR	42 million each year	25 million each year
ACREAGE	843	1,017
NUMBER OF SIDES ABUTTING AN OCEAN	0	1
NUMBER OF DAYS EACH YEAR WITH GREEN TREES, GRASS, AND BLOOMING FLOWERS	approx. 230	365
NUMBER OF TREES	18,000	more than 130,000
NUMBER OF LAKES AND PONDS	8	11
CAR-FREE STREETS	6 miles	4.4 miles

The park proved wildly popular by the turn of the century. *(Photo courtesy of Greg Gaar)*

"Golden Gate Park now appears to be the objective point of nearly all out-of-door pleasure-seekers," Hall wrote in a report to the park commission. "It must be admitted that the improvement of the Park is supplying a great public necessity."

Even if there was a bit of humble-bragging in his report, Hall deserved every word. He had dramatically transformed the landscape in record time, firmly establishing his vision for it. Sadly, a small group of park-haters wanted to cut off funds for the park. They made false accusations of Hall that made his job miserable enough that he resigned as superintendent in 1876. But thankfully, Hall advised on park matters for several years, during which time he was part of a crucial decision: hiring John McLaren as assistant superintendent in 1887. And while Hall wasn't in charge anymore, he would get to see the park succeed in a big way. By 1895, it had more than half a million visits each year in a city with a population of 325,000.

The John McLaren Years: 1887–1943

Scotsman John McLaren got hired as assistant superintendent of Golden Gate Park in 1887, thanks to the name he'd made for himself as a master gardener in the San Francisco Bay Area. Fifteen years earlier, McLaren immigrated to the United States after being hired by a wealthy American who wanted to make his estate in San Mateo look like a European park. He succeeded there and at other prominent people's gardens in the region.

McLaren had been a paid gardener since he was fourteen. "Work and life in a garden were the nicest things I could think of as a boy, and I've never changed my mind," McLaren said toward the end of his life. Although he took some botany classes at the Royal Botanic Garden in Edinburgh as a young man, he was mostly self-taught (like Hall). McLaren is said to have had an uncanny understanding of nature, as well as a deep appreciation of it. "Why must people change beautiful things?" he would say.

As the park's assistant superintendent from 1887 to 1890, McLaren was tasked with landscaping the new Sharon Quarters for Children (now the Koret Children's Quarter) and continuing Hall's work overseeing the planting of tens of thousands of trees. McLaren must have proved himself as more than just an excellent gardener, and in 1890 he became superintendent. At the time, the park was still a work in progress. There were also plenty of powerful people who had their own ideas about development in the park, many of whom were not aligned with creating an escape into nature.

One of these was journalist, businessman, and *San Francisco Chronicle* founder Michael Henry de Young. De Young wanted to host a World's Fair in the park to further put San Francisco on the map and boost the economy, and McLaren reluctantly had to get on board. The resulting California Midwinter International Exposition of 1894—a "World's Fair"—ended up being one of two big boom times for park development.

The buildings and complexes quickly built in 1893 forever shaped the area that's now the Music Concourse. It's why the de Young Museum, California Academy of Sciences, and Japanese Tea Garden are in this part of the park, along with some of the sculptures and even the wooden benches you can still find in the Concourse today. McLaren also had Blue Heron Lake, the Rustic Bridge, and the Roman Bridge completed just in time for the California Midwinter Expo. Huntington Falls, which

McLaren was inspired to build after a trip to the Sierra Nevada with conservationist John Muir, was completed before the Expo ended.

Meanwhile, McLaren would stop at nothing to realize his vision of a verdant park. He had the first windmill (the Dutch) built to pump water for plant irrigation. He had the artificial dune across from Ocean Beach further built up: the park's essential windbreak (especially for young trees). Special train cars brought vast amounts of street sweepings—i.e., manure—from downtown to improve the soil. Sewage water was used for irrigation on the western end of the park until neighbors complained too much. McLaren also designed the Chain of Lakes. There was no moss growing under this gardener's feet!

When San Francisco's devastating earthquake happened on April 18, 1906, McLaren then had to manage a park-turned-refugee-camp (see sidebar). Somehow, in the midst of overseeing disaster recovery logistics and the repair of many damaged park buildings, McLaren taught children living in the refugee camps how to garden. Once the camps were removed and McLaren was back to making his horticultural dreams a reality, Michael Henry de Young proposed the 1915 World's Fair be held in the park. This time, however, McLaren put his foot down. (The

The 1894 California Midwinter Expo led to a surge of park development, including completing Blue Heron Lake, the Roman Bridge, and the Rustic Bridge shown here. *(Photo by Robert Ho)*

The Music Concourse, including many of its inviting wooden benches, is a remnant of the 1894 California Midwinter Expo. *(Photo by Jim Watkins)*

Panama-Pacific International Exposition would be held in what's now the Marina neighborhood instead.) McLaren's efforts to protect the original vision for the park continued. When Kezar Stadium and Pavilion were built in the mid-1920s, McLaren fought for these to take up the least amount of park land possible (and he got 3 acres of land added to the park as part of the deal, bringing the park up to 1,017 acres). As cars increasingly encroached on the park, McLaren wouldn't have potholes fixed in order to slow down drivers.

McLaren's tenure included the Great Depression as well, which started in 1929. This dark time in the city and nation led to the park's second building boom. When

President Franklin D. Roosevelt started the Works Progress Administration in 1935 to create much-needed jobs, local workers built the Anglers Lodge and casting pools, the Model Yacht Clubhouse, and the horse stables. The park got some upgrades and repairs, plus art projects like the murals in Beach Chalet. It was also during this era that McLaren established the tree-lighting tradition outside his home in the park.

Through it all, McLaren continued above all else to be what he called the "boss gardener" of the park. He designed gardens, dells, and forests with diverse species from around the world numbering in the tens of thousands. He pushed relentlessly for an arboretum (today's Botanical Garden at Strybing Arboretum) which

A Refugee Camp in the Aftermath of the 1906 Earthquake

About two-thirds of San Francisco's residents lost their homes after the great earthquake on the morning of April 18, 1906. In the immediate aftermath, Golden Gate Park became a temporary sanctuary for around 200,000 people. These numbers soon dropped to about 40,000, with people housed in tents in the Panhandle, around the Children's Quarter, near the Conservatory of Flowers, in the Big Rec Ball Field, and in Speedway Meadow (now called Hellman Hollow). Many wounded were cared for in what's now called Robin Williams Meadow.

Refugees of the Great Earthquake of 1906, including many children, lived in the park until January 1907. *(Photo courtesy of Greg Gaar)*

John McLaren, who was the superintendent of not just Golden Gate Park but *all* San Francisco parks, played a large role in deciding what to do about longer-term refugee housing. He even gave the final say on what the mass-produced "earthquake shacks"—small wooden structures—would look like.

Though earthquake shacks were put in many San Francisco parks, none went in Golden Gate Park. But it's not because McLaren said earthquake refugee camps were "a harbor for thieves and vagabonds and full of disease and crime." (Yes, he did say that!) The park was just too far away from downtown and where the jobs were.

took decades to realize. He's credited with overseeing the planting of hundreds of thousands of trees in the park—and two million citywide.

McLaren did all this while stubbornly defending the park from being overdeveloped, with some strategic compromises. The fact that he stayed in the job so long is another testament to his abilities. The public loved the park and they loved McLaren—and that popularity protected him politically. A city charter was changed so he could continue past the mandatory retirement age, which was seventy at the time. McLaren would die at age ninety-six after more than half a century on the job, still the superintendent, at his home in the park (now called McLaren Lodge). Ultimately, William Hammond Hall chose exactly the right person to realize his original vision for the park—and then some. Thank goodness.

A Hero of the Park: Sue Bierman

As you stand under some of the Panhandle's giant trees, imagine if there were instead eight lanes of high-speed traffic zooming along a sunken open-air tunnel—and all the Victorian houses in sight were *gone*. It could easily have happened. As freeway expansions destroyed countless neighborhoods across America in the 1950s and 1960s, a proposed Panhandle Freeway was dangerously close to being built.

We have Sue Bierman to thank for this awful idea finally being defeated in 1966—failing by just one vote among the board of supervisors (cast by City Supervisor Jack Morrison). Bierman was an activist who led a campaign, mostly composed of mothers and other women, to fight the freeway for eight years! You'll find benches, a plaque, and a circle of trees tucked in the Panhandle (at Shrader Street) dedicated to Bierman. For her tenacious activism and community organizing to protect the park and its surrounding neighborhoods, Sue Bierman is a Golden Gate Park hero.

Post-McLaren Period

McLaren's long tenure meant that by the time of his death in 1943, much of what we know and love about the park today was well-established. In fact, the remainder of the twentieth century brought few major changes. There were times when some icons of the park could have been lost forever. The Dutch and Murphy Windmills fell into such disrepair that the fate of each of the "San Francisco Giants" was in question at different times. In 1995, a storm with winds of up to 100 miles per hour shattered half of the 60,000 panes of glass in the Conservatory of Flowers—and the possibility of tearing down this treasure was all too real. (Activism and fundraising saved all three structures.)

Other threats to the park were narrowly averted, including a terrible plan that emerged in the 1950s to turn the Panhandle and abutting blocks into an eight-lane sunken freeway. This project would have also taken out the northeastern corner of the park to connect the Central Freeway downtown to Park Presidio and then to the Golden Gate Bridge (see sidebar on p. 22).

This era of the park included the San Francisco 49ers playing in Kezar Stadium from 1946 to 1971. In the 1960s, the park became the backdrop—and also a launching pad—for the counterculture movement and some of the defining music that went with it. Janis Joplin and Jimi Hendrix played in the Panhandle. In 1967, tens of thousands of people gathered in the Polo Field for the Human Be-In, which featured speakers like Timothy Leary and Allen Ginsberg and performances by the Grateful Dead and Jefferson Airplane. Then there was the roller-skating craze

The park was the backdrop and stage for major music and cultural moments, especially in the 1960s and 1970s. Jerry Garcia (shown here in 1974 with dancer Renee Ballister) and the Grateful Dead were a big part of that. *(Photo courtesy of Greg Gaar)*

of the 1970s, with tens of thousands of people on eight wheels descending on the park during the weekends.

The 1980s was a darker period, with the city's crown jewel tarnishing a bit as it got run-down, overgrown, and even dangerous at times. The park reflected some of the broader challenges the city was facing with civil unrest and crime, and it suffered from underinvestment and neglect. Another setback was in 1989, when the Loma Prieta earthquake took a serious toll on the aging California Academy of Sciences and the de Young Museum buildings.

The Panhandle

The one-block-wide-by-eight-block-long stretch of green called the Panhandle was once a grand driveway for Golden Gate Park. Originally called "The Avenue," its winding paths were for horse-drawn carriages (and automobiles from 1913 to 1955). But the Panhandle doesn't just lead *to* Golden Gate Park—it's been part of the park since its creation in 1870. A surprising amount of history has happened in this thin stretch of green.

First, the names of the streets running from north to south along the Panhandle explain part of its history. Stanyan, Shrader, Cole, Clayton, and Ashbury Streets are named for the five members of the Outside Lands Committee, who secured the land acquisition for the park (including the Panhandle) from homesteaders and squatters. Note that the committee *wasn't* totally successful: the original plans had the Panhandle as wide as the park, but that didn't happen in the compromise they forged.

The Panhandle was the first place in the park where trees were planted. This means many of the towering Monterey cypress, Monterey pine, and blue gum eucalyptus trees you see are likely approaching 150 years old and are even bigger than the trees in the rest of the park. Mike Sullivan's book *The Trees of San Francisco* includes an excellent walking tour of notable Panhandle trees.

President Theodore Roosevelt visited the Panhandle in 1904 to dedicate the William McKinley Memorial, which is at the Baker Street end of the Panhandle (Roosevelt succeeded McKinley after McKinley was assassinated in 1901). Roosevelt's trip to California included—very importantly—a trip to Yosemite with John Muir, which influenced Roosevelt's rapid expansion of our national parks and monuments.

The Panhandle was also the site of some defining moments of the 1960s counterculture movement. On

Yet the park offered light, beauty, and refuge. It was in the 1980s, as San Francisco reeled from the AIDS epidemic, that people started talking about having a dedicated space to grieve and remember those who died from AIDS (more on p. 86). Later, the park would become home to the first and only federal AIDS memorial.

The Panhandle is officially part of Golden Gate Park. Its giant trees, the oldest in the park, make this narrow stretch of land a green oasis.

October 6, 1966, hundreds gathered for a "Love Pageant Rally" to protest LSD becoming illegal, with performances by the Grateful Dead and Big Brother and the Holding Company featuring Janis Joplin. On June 25, 1967, Jimi Hendrix kicked off the Summer of Love when he played a free concert on the north side of the Panhandle near Ashbury Street off the back of a truck.

Today, the Panhandle is a well-used space for outdoor fitness classes, youth soccer practices, slacklining, dog walking, and more. The busiest areas are clustered around Clayton Street and include fitness equipment stations, the Nate Thurmond Panhandle Basketball Courts (see p. 110), and the Panhandle Playground (see p. 94).

Although significant vehicle traffic on the abutting Oak and Fell Streets makes the Panhandle less peaceful than the park itself, it's worth exploring. It's also proof of the immeasurable value of every bit of park space in a city. It's a shame that an 1899 proposal to extend the Panhandle all the way to the heart of San Francisco didn't happen.

A New Century

The twenty-first century brought a new golden era for the park, with many improvements, investments, and events. The new de Young Museum opened in 2005, the new Koret Children's Quarter playground in 2007, the new California Academy of Sciences in 2008, the new Lisa and Douglas Goldman Tennis Center in 2021, and the renovated golf course and new golf course clubhouse in 2023. All of these have brought a shine to the park and attracted more visitors. Yet none of these changes have dramatically altered the park, preserving its timeless feel.

The park has also gotten needed resources. Voters passed measures to fund city parks in 2008, 2012, and 2020. You can see the results in projects like the Panhandle Playground, Middle Lake, the oak woodlands trails, and the Haight Street entrance. The park is incredibly clean and green; you can feel the pride that both paid and volunteer gardeners have in their work. Individual donors are also investing in the park.

There is more music than ever. Three annual music festivals were started: Hardly Strictly Bluegrass in 2001, Outside Lands in 2008, and Flower Piano in 2015. The Bandshell and JFK Promenade are regularly alive with music, and long-running free concerts like Opera in the Park continue.

There are now 4-plus miles of car-free and low-traffic streets, including JFK Promenade (more on p. 88). This change has brought the park closer to the original vision for it, by allowing visitors to enjoy more of the park without dangerous vehicle traffic. As the park's "Main Street," JFK Promenade is now a space for community instead of a cut-through for cars.

Today, there are more gardens than ever and park staff are planting more native species than ever. Pipevine swallowtail butterflies are back, Nuttall's white-crowned sparrows are nesting, and great blue herons are everywhere. The Phil Arnold Trail in the oak woodlands opened in 2019, and restoration efforts have created a fifty-acre biodiversity hotspot.

If you want to feel better about the world, just visit Golden Gate Park—it's the best of the best. I fell in love with the park two decades ago. But I fell in love all over again during the global pandemic that started in 2020. The park provided an essential and restorative refuge for the city's people. It was a saving grace for my young kids, who could climb trees and ride bikes when their schools and the playgrounds were closed. With 1,017 acres, we never got bored—ever. The park was there for us. It always is, for everyone.

Here's to you, William Hammond Hall and John McLaren.

A Local's Park

What would San Francisco be without Golden Gate Park? What would my *life* be without Golden Gate Park? In 2007, I moved with my husband to an apartment one block from Golden Gate Park. We'd already lived in the city for a couple of years, and truthfully, I hadn't bonded with it yet. San Francisco was so different from where I'd lived before, especially where I'd grown up in the Midwest. But with every visit to the park, this changed. The park was increasingly where much of our life happened. Walks, runs, endless free concerts, barbeques with new friends. Every time I crossed Kezar Drive and headed down the path into the park's embrace, I felt more at home in the city.

When we had our first kid in 2012, the park revealed all kinds of new wonders—including the revelation that our infant daughter would stop crying if we went there. I spent countless hours pushing a stroller in the park, had some memorable diaper changes, and soon was logging dozens of visits to the California Academy of Sciences. Somewhere along the way I started writing an A-to-Z book to see if I could find something for each letter that was truly unique about Golden Gate Park. Eventually, I did! My children's book *Golden Gate Park, An A to Z Adventure* came out in 2020, timed with the 150th anniversary of the park.

When the opportunity to write this guidebook came about, I had to do it. I mean, when you're in love, you want to tell people about it, right? For me, learning about the park's past makes the present that much richer. Plus, I get a rush of happiness discovering and sharing the best park secrets. Whether you're a local or visiting from elsewhere, I want you to have the *best* time. Because I really believe it's the *best* park.

TEN FUN FACTS about Golden Gate Park

1 The public did not originally support the park's location on what was at the time referred to as the "Great Sand Bank." It was considered too far from where people lived, and no one could imagine the large dunes could become a lush park.

2 Contrary to a common misconception, the park was *not* designed by architect Frederick Law Olmsted, who designed New York City's Central Park with Calvert Vaux. Golden Gate Park was designed by William Hammond Hall.

3 The first public playground in the United States was built in what's now called the Koret Children's Quarter. There were swings, slides, seesaws, and . . . goat cart rides!

4 Bison have lived in the park since 1891. The captive breeding program here helped bring bison back from the brink of extinction in the United States.

5 The park served as a refugee camp and hospital after the great earthquake on April 18, 1906, providing homes for 40,000 people for several months.

6 The first movie shot in the park was filmed in 1914. The following year, the biggest movie star of the era, Charlie Chaplin, filmed *A Jitney Elopement* there (you can watch it on YouTube). But the most famous movie shot in the park was probably the classic *Dirty Harry*, starring Clint Eastwood.

7 The sand dunes the park was built on are made of granite sand washed down from the Sierra Nevada and shaped into hills by Pacific winds over thousands of years.

8 The park has two windmills, initially built to pump water for irrigating the park: the Dutch and the Murphy. Each year the Murphy's sails take a spin on King's Day.

9 The fortune cookie you get at the end of a Chinese meal was invented at the Japanese Tea Garden by Makoto Hagiwara, who designed and cared for the garden for decades.

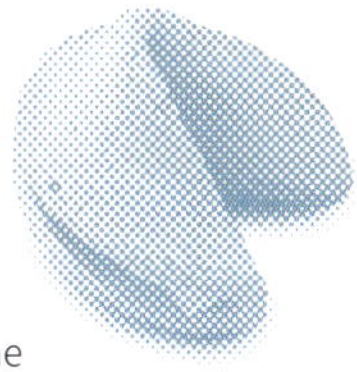

10 Golden Gate Park is 2.5 miles from the Golden Gate Bridge. Both were named for the "Golden Gate Strait," the mile-wide entrance to the San Francisco Bay. On a clear day, you can see the bridge from various points in the park.

Left to right: William Hammond Hall was just 24 when he designed Golden Gate Park *(Photo courtesy of The Bancroft Library, UC, Berkeley)*; bison were first brought to the park for a Wild West feel *(Photo by Jim Watkins)*; some people call the two windmills the San Francisco Giants *(Photo by Robert Ho)*; stop by the Japanese Tea House for a fortune cookie *(Photo by Jim Watkins)*; fortune cookie *(Photo by Kasia Derenda)*

How to Use This Book

Golden Gate Park, whether you visit once or countless times, always offers more than meets the eye. Even in the busiest parts of the park, there are secluded spots where you can be immersed in nature. Then there are those experiences of awe awaiting you, whether they take the form of a beautiful painting, bird, or bloom. The park can also be a place for human connection, from people-watching on JFK Promenade to finding "your people" anywhere from a skating rink to a rock concert.

Map Legend

1	State highway		Landmark
	Surface street		Bridge
	Car-free street		Gate
	Walk route		Fence
	Other paths and trails		Hilltop
	Stairs		Building
	Walk number		Stream
T	Start (Trailhead)		Body of water
1	Parking		Falls
	Restrooms and water		Shuttle route/stop
	Drinking fountain	N	Muni light rail
	Picnic table	5R	Muni bus route
	View/overlook		Park/preserve
	Bench		Athletic fields/venues
N	North		Woodland/grove
			Other land

Opposite: Like the nesting great blue herons each spring, you can count on the beauty and solace the park provides. *(Photo by Robert Ho)*

Going in search of all of the park's waterfalls will take you to some of the most spectacular areas; see p. 175 for a full list. *(Photo by Jim Watkins)*

This book will help you have more of those moments that make your visit to the park *more*. Here's some guidance on how to get the *most* more.

Choose a walk or hike to expand your horizons. The walks and hikes range from short and accessible to hilly hikes or trails traversing the length of the park. If you're new to the park, any of the hikes on the eastern end are easy to get to; plus, they include classic sights and will get you off the beaten path. If you know the eastern half of the park well, pick a west side hike and see if you discover something new.

If you're visiting with kids, I've got you covered. My kids were practically raised in the park, so the recommendations and advice in this book are ground tested. Be sure to read through the Playgrounds section (p. 94) and the details for any major attraction you want to go to (especially the California Academy of Sciences). There are also a couple of especially family-friendly hikes: **Roses and Redwoods** and **Medieval Monastery Stones**), and of course you should read about fairy doors on p. 103. My children's book, *Golden Gate Park: An A to Z Adventure*, is a great companion for little ones, too.

If you love music, tune in to a couple of key sections. The park's musical offerings are off the charts, and you may want to plan your visit around this. Read about the music festivals and the range of free offerings at various locations on p. 100.

Take in the park's history amid park history. McLaren Lodge, the Sharon Art Building, and the Conservatory of Flowers all date back to Victorian times. Find a bench near one of these buildings and read the first section for a short deep-dive into the park's 150-plus year history.

Know before you go. You can't go wrong in the park, but there are insider tips that can take your experience from good to great. Whatever attraction or activity you've chosen, I recommend using the index to find and read the related content beforehand.

VISITING THE PARK

At 1,017 acres, the sheer size of Golden Gate Park means there is a lot to know about getting around—and getting the most out of it. This section will help you with all the ins-and-outs, whether you're a first-time visitor or longtime fan. If nothing else, just be sure to bring a jacket!

Opposite: *The Japanese Tea Garden is just the right scale for young children to enjoy exploring, and the Moon Bridge is always a hit.*

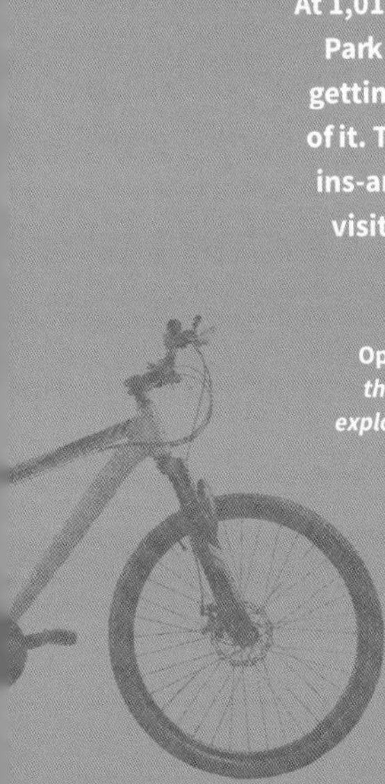

Rules and Regulations

The park rules and regulations ensure a safe and pleasant time for all visitors. Hours are from 5 a.m. to midnight, and overnight parking is prohibited. The speed limit within the park's boundaries is 25 mph, except for Crossover Drive, which is 35 mph. Dogs must be on leash, except in designated off-leash areas (see p. 47 for more on visiting with dogs). Pick up and remove dog waste, and prevent digging and/or other destructive behavior. Fires, firearms, other weapons, and fireworks are prohibited, as are drones without a permit. Do not feed or bother wildlife of any kind. Collecting or removing any material from inside the park, including rocks, flowers, and artifacts, is prohibited.

Park code states that alcohol is prohibited in playground areas, the greater Robin Williams Meadow area, Kezar Stadium and the surrounding area, and the Panhandle. That means alcohol *is* allowed in the vast majority of the park. But park code also states that anyone intoxicated with liquor, drugs, or controlled substances who is threatening their own or others' safety can be removed. Smoking is prohibited.

The park is enjoyable at night, too, especially along JFK Promenade. Every night, a light show is projected onto the sides of the Conservatory of Flowers. *(Photo by Jim Watkins)*

To report a maintenance or vandalism issue in the park, call 311 or go to sf311.org. If you're local, download the 311 app to report incidents using your phone's GPS capability to pinpoint the location so that park staff can easily locate and address the problem. For example, if you find a big pile of trash on a remote trail, pinpoint and mark the location in your report. Staff appreciate these location-specific reports in part because the park is so large. To reach San Francisco Recreation & Parks rangers, call (415) 242-6390. For crime-related calls and emergencies, call 911 or the San Francisco Police Department Park Police Station at (415) 242-3000.

Golden Gate Park at Night

The park is open until midnight, and the east side still has plenty of visitors after dark. JFK Promenade stays busy well into the evening with bike commuters, runners, and people strolling. (Lights and reflectors are strongly recommended on what can be a very dark street.) The year-round nightly light show displayed on the Conservatory of Flowers is a great reason to visit the park after dark, and in recent years, there have been wintertime light installations on JFK Promenade.

The Goldman Tennis Center's courts are lit up until 10 p.m., as are the soccer fields at the Beach Chalet Athletic Fields. The California Academy of Sciences hosts a weekly event for adults aged twenty-one and up on Thursday evenings called NightLife, and the Blue Heron Boathouse becomes a music venue on many weekends. The park at night is worth experiencing, especially the quiet in a big city (with an occasional hoot of a great horned owl). Use good judgment, bring a flashlight, and stay in more trafficked parts of the park vs. dark forests), but don't be afraid to enjoy the park in the dark.

Transportation

Unlike Central Park in New York City, Golden Gate Park isn't very central. However, there are many options for getting to the park, especially to the many attractions on the eastern end. There are also a variety of ways to get around the park once you're there. Leave the car behind if you can; it allows you much more flexibility in exploring.

Muni (Public Transit)

Golden Gate Park is well served by public transportation both with buses and light rail. In fact, according to the San Francisco Municipal Transportation Agency (which runs Muni), 70 percent of San Franciscans are within a fifteen-minute walk of a transfer-free Muni ride to Golden Gate Park.

The 5, 5R (Rapid), 7, 18, 28, 28R, 29, 33, and 44 Muni bus routes all offer direct service to Golden Gate Park. The 6, 31, and 43 Muni bus routes and the N Judah light rail line all have stops within a ten-minute walk of the park. The N Judah light rail line runs frequently about two blocks away from the park's southern edge. The 5 and 5R bus lines run along the entire north side of the park on Fulton Street (and go downtown), also with frequent service. This means you can hike through the park, get tired, and just head north or south to be rescued by an N Judah, 5, or 5R that will take you to the eastern end of the park or downtown.

You can plan your route using Google Maps. For the latest options for how to pay your fare, go to sfmta.com/fares.

Park Shuttle

This free shuttle is provided by San Francisco Recreation & Parks daily year-round. The shuttle serves all major attractions on the eastern end of the park, is wheelchair accessible, and has stops near or at most of the Muni routes serving Golden Gate Park. Most of the routes and stops are along JFK Promenade, which does not allow private vehicles. You can get on and off at any designated shuttle stop.

If you're looking for a direct connection from a Muni bus to the shuttle, the shuttle shares a stop at the intersection of Haight and Stanyan Streets with the 7 and the 33 Muni bus lines. The shuttle also shares stops with the 44 Muni bus line on the Music Concourse. **For daily hours and the full route, visit sfrecpark.org.** The Golden Gate Park Shuttle is also integrated into Google Maps and will show up as an option if you select "transit."

Private Tour Buses

Some people visit Golden Gate Park as a stop on one of the hop-on/hop-off buses or other private tours. These buses typically drop people off at the Music Concourse, which is a good starting point for many of the park's attractions.

Bicycling Through the Park to the Pacific on Car-Free Routes

One of the best things to do in the park—and in fact, the entire city—is to ride a bike across the entire park to the ocean on a route that is almost completely free of cars. Except for a few brief sections and intersections, you will enjoy open streets, no vehicle traffic, and big smiles (plus many of the classic sights and some hidden treasures) as you pedal along this 3.3-mile route.

Starting from the east where Kezar Drive and JFK Promenade meet, ride JFK Promenade for about 1.5 miles. Then at Transverse Drive, take a left and then immediately take a right onto Overlook Drive. After about 0.3 mile on Overlook, continue west on Middle Drive West for 0.8 mile, then merge onto MLK Drive and continue west for about 0.7 mile until you hit Lincoln Way and the ocean is in sight.

See p. 112 for a map of this slow-traffic route. Google Maps won't necessarily offer this option and may instead suggest riding JFK Drive on the western half of the park, which can have a lot of car traffic. I'm always sad to see both tourists and locals unknowingly take that route.

I highly recommend continuing to ride south along the ocean for 2 miles. This new car-free promenade and park, called Sunset Dunes, opened in 2025. Combining this with the car-free and low-traffic streets in Golden Gate Park, you can now do a spectacular 10-mile-roundtrip bike ride with almost no traffic.

This bike route connects the 1.5-mile JFK Promenade (shown here) to Sunset Dunes, a two-mile park along the Pacific Ocean.

Bicycling

Golden Gate Park is a biking destination for cyclists of all ages and abilities, thanks to its safe, scenic routes, including many without vehicle traffic, like JFK Promenade. To get to Golden Gate Park on a bike, use Google Maps and select "bicycle" to see routes to the park that usually avoid hills and incorporate bike lanes. Page Street, which is one of the city's low-traffic "Slow Streets," is a safe and pleasant way to bike to the park, as is the Panhandle. Arguello Boulevard is another major bike route from the north side of the city to Golden Gate Park.

Outdoor bike racks are plentiful and are scattered around the park and at all major attractions. There are especially large numbers of racks by the Bandshell on the Music Concourse. The most secure bike parking is inside the Music Concourse garage and in the Goldman Tennis Center, but generally bikes are safe to leave locked (using a high-quality lock) in the park during the daytime. Large events in the park typically provide temporary racks for bike parking and/or bike valet parking.

Bicyclists are not allowed on sidewalks, except for children under the age of thirteen. Please note that there are many paths where bikes are not allowed, which are marked directly on the path. There is also a growing network of multiuse paths, made up of both single-track and dirt roads, where off-road cycling, or mountain biking, is allowed (learn more on p. 112).

In terms of bicyclist etiquette, pass other cyclists on the left. When passing people who are on foot, give them plenty of space and go slow, especially when passing young children and people with disabilities.

BIKESHARE AND BIKE RENTAL

If you want to experience a lot of the park in a day and get into the less-visited west side, bicycles are the best way. You have a couple of options if you need to rent a bike. There are bike rental companies near the park (and one inside the park), which usually charge a flat fee for a whole day in the park. Helmets and locks are provided by the companies. Both pedal- and electric-powered bikes are usually offered, and some companies also lead guided bicycle tours.

There are also bikeshare stations near and in the park. You can download the Bay Wheels app to rent one of these pedal- or electric-powered bikes for either one ride or for the day; fees vary. One advantage about bikesharing is you can park the bike in a different station than where you started, or even pay extra to leave it at any city bike rack. Learn more at baywheels.com.

Surreys, Segways, and Scooters

If you're looking for a less traditional way to explore the park, there are some options. You can rent a two- or four-person **surrey**, where all passengers pedal what is essentially a large bicycle buggy. These surreys start from behind the Bandshell on the Music Concourse and at the Haight and Stanyan entrance of the park, depending on the day of the week. They are generally one-hour rides, so think of it as a fun activity rather than a means of transportation. Departing from the Bandshell offers a more varied route; however, pedaling and navigating a surrey is easiest on the flat stretch of JFK Promenade east of 8th Avenue.

You sometimes see **Segways** in the park—two-wheeled, stand-up, self-balancing scooters. Usually they are part of guided group tours, which is the safest and most reputable way to try a Segway. How much of the park you'll see and what

Surreys, which can be rented by the hour, are one of many ways to get around the park. Be sure your quads are ready and avoid any hills!

you'll learn on these tours varies. Segways are prohibited on sidewalks, but they are allowed on multimodal paths marked okay for bicycles.

When it comes to electric scooters, the options are constantly changing. If you're arriving on a two-wheeled, stand-up **e-scooter**, it's just like riding a bike around the park. You can ride on JFK Promenade, bike lanes on other park roads, and multiuse paths, but stay off sidewalks (it's illegal). However, if you're using a **mobility scooter**, you can be anywhere. If you are visiting from out of town, you can rent mobility scooters through online sites.

Driving

Have to drive to the park? Here are some helpful things to know before you go, whether it's in your vehicle or you're being dropped off or picked up.

Private vehicles (including cars, SUVs, trucks, motorcycles, mopeds) are prohibited on JFK Promenade (from Kezar Drive to Transverse Drive), Conservatory Drive East and most of Conservatory Drive West, Overlook Drive, a section of Middle Drive West, and a short section of MLK Drive from 41st to 49th Avenues. These permanent vehicle closures are shown in Google Maps or similar navigation tools.

Chain of Lakes Drive is used as a cut-through of the park by some drivers, and it can get very backed up during rush hour and on weekends, as can 9th Avenue (which becomes MLK Drive) and Transverse Drive. If you can, avoid driving to the park if you want to save money and avoid stress.

The Music Concourse garage at 55 Hagiwara Tea Garden Drive is a paid, secure, eight-hundred-space underground parking garage that has direct access to the de Young Museum and the California Academy of Sciences and is convenient to many park destinations. The garage has two entrances: the north entrance of the garage at Fulton Street and 10th Avenue, and the south entrance on Music Concourse Drive at MLK Drive inside the park. The garage has thirty-three ADA spots that are within 150 feet of direct entrances to the de Young Museum and California Academy of Sciences. This garage is open from 7 a.m. to 7 p.m., though it is sometimes open later for special events. Go to sfmta.com/garages-lots/music-concourse-garage to learn more.

The Kezar parking lot at 825 Stanyan Street is a lesser-known parking lot in the very southeast corner of the park. It is open 24/7 but has limited capacity. Learn more at sfmta.com. If this lot is full, the University of California San Francisco

Millberry Union public garage at 500 Parnassus Avenue is a good backup that's just two blocks from the park.

SURFACE PARKING LOTS

You'll find free, small parking lots (all of which have ADA spaces) within the park at the San Francisco Lawn Bowling Club, the Blue Heron Boathouse, the Golden Gate Park Dog Training Area, the Golden Gate Angling & Casting Club, the Beach Chalet Athletic Fields, Beach Chalet, and Chain of Lakes Meadow. There is very limited, free two-hour parking around and in front of McLaren Lodge, but it is intended mostly for park staff rather than the public. It is not recommended during business hours, except for the ADA spaces.

ON-STREET PARKING

There is free parking from 5 a.m. to midnight on many roads within the park, as well as the streets bordering the north and south sides of the park: Fulton Street, Lincoln Way, and Kezar Drive. Parking generally ranges from two to four hours. The farther west you go in the park, the easier parking *usually* is. But on beautiful weekends or during special events, all bets are off. A word of caution: Do not leave ANY belongings visible in your vehicle. Thieves can break into cars within minutes, and this is not the kind of memory you want to make in Golden Gate Park.

RECOMMENDED PASSENGER DROP-OFF AND PICK-UP AREAS

There are many entrances to the park, but some are better than others for dropping off or picking up passengers. This also applies to locations for taxi or rideshare pick-up and drop-off.

The most convenient locations on the eastern end of the park are:

- At designated loading zones in the Music Concourse
- In the parking area next to the Lawn Bowling Club at 320 Bowling Green Drive
- At the red-curbed loading zone on Fulton Street by Park Presidio Boulevard between the bus stop and the ADA parking area
- At designated loading zones on 9th Avenue in front of the San Francisco County Fair Building
- Behind the Conservatory of Flowers via Arguello Boulevard

The park continues to become more accessible, with more ways for people with disabilities or mobility limitations to get around.

ACCESSIBILITY

If you are dropping off someone with limited mobility who needs to be able to get directly onto the free Golden Gate Park Shuttle, your best drop-off spots are the following locations:

- In front of McLaren Lodge (501 Stanyan Street)
- The free ADA parking lot behind the Bandshell on the Music Concourse (75 Hagiwara Tea Drive); additional paid ADA parking is available nearby in the Music Concourse garage
- The Blue Heron Boathouse (50 Blue Heron Lake Drive)

San Francisco Recreation & Parks hosts a free adaptive bicycling program on Saturdays for people with disabilities (currently summer through early fall). The program matches people with disabilities to adaptive bicycles by advance reservation, which are provided by the Bay Area Outreach and Recreation Program (BORP). Options include handcycles, recumbent bikes, side-by-side tandems, and more. Learn more at borp.org.

There are ADA parking spaces throughout the park. A complete map of these can be found at sfrecpark.org. A map of Golden Gate Park's most usable pathways for people with disabilities is linked at sfrecpark.org/1159/Getting-to-Golden-Gate-Park and can help you find paths that are smooth and without significant inclines. For all major attractions in the book, accessibility and ADA parking are described.

Weather: Wind and Fog

Before Golden Gate Park was created, it was home to massive sand dunes—sixty to one hundred feet tall! They were created by the winds barreling eastward off the Pacific Ocean. While William Hammond Hall and John McLaren did a masterful job shaping dunes and planting trees to create windbreaks, it can still be very windy.

In San Francisco, the wind is often coming at you in the form of fog, with all its bone-chilling dampness and view-blocking gloom. Summer is the foggiest time of year, as higher temperatures and lower air densities inland suck cold, dense air from the ocean across Golden Gate Park and through the Golden Gate itself. Note that in the summer, the fog and wind are usually at their worst in the afternoon and early evening.

Some of San Francisco's hills can block the fog from reaching other parts of the city, which is why you could be enjoying the sun downtown with no clue that the fog has enshrouded Golden Gate Park. But you can find out about conditions at websites fog.today, sfsunset.today, and fogcam.org.

It's best to dress in layers when you go to Golden Gate Park. There can be big temperature differences

Don't let most of the photos in this book fool you. It's often cold, gray, and windy in the park. *(Photo by Robert Ho)*

Where Can You See the Golden Gate Bridge?

If it isn't too foggy, here are a few places you can go to catch a glimpse of the iconic Golden Gate Bridge:

- The Hamon Observation Tower at the de Young Museum
- The top of Strawberry Hill on Blue Heron Lake
- The top of the hill behind the Conservatory of Flowers, at the intersection of Arguello Boulevard and Conservatory Drive, and near the Breast Cancer Memorial Garden
- Many spots along the **Northern Edge** hike (see p. 199)

depending on where you are in the park. Meteorologist Mike Pechner found that one of the coldest spots in San Francisco is Golden Gate Park. Called Fulton Hollow by Pechner, this sunken area collects cold air in the oak woodlands in the northeasternmost corner of the park. Pechner says you'll even find frost here in the winter—very rare for San Francisco.

If you're looking for warmer spots in the park with less blustery wind, seek out areas to the east of the park's hills or in depressions (though fog can sit in those spots). The 14th Avenue East Meadow off of JFK Promenade is often warmer, as are the somewhat-sunken Hellman Hollow picnic area and Heroes Grove. Peacock Meadow, near the Conservatory of Flowers, has a big stand of trees that blocks the wind, making it somewhat warmer than in front of the Conservatory if it's gusty there. Generally, the eastern half of the park is warmer than the west side. And if you're freezing, visit the Conservatory of Flowers—it's always tropical inside.

Restrooms

If you're spending a day in the park, finding public restrooms is crucial. But the park is big enough that you won't always be close to one. Note that Google Maps does *not* show all public restrooms, but the map on p. 8 does.

Looking for a public all-gender restroom? There aren't many, but they do exist. You'll find one at the Flywheel Coffee kiosk next to the bocce courts, at McLaren Lodge, in the Goldman Tennis Center, at the Boat Playground at 45th Avenue, on the lowest level of the de Young Museum, and at the golf course clubhouse.

Want the nicest public restrooms in the park? The restrooms at the Goldman Tennis Center and the golf course clubhouse are tops, followed by the ones at the de Young Museum (note that you can use the ones on the lower and main floors without buying a ticket). Most restrooms have a diaper changing table.

Dogs

There's an oft-repeated line in San Francisco: "There are more dogs than children." The most recent census data confirms this is true. There are likely more than 200,000 dogs in the city, and you'll see plenty in the park, with practically a daily doggie parade on JFK Promenade.

The **Golden Gate Park Dog Training Area** (969 36th Avenue will get you there on Google Maps) is the largest fenced-in dog park in the city, with areas for big and small dogs—plus views of the nearby bison. A $2.4 million renovation was completed in 2021, which local dog owners helped design. It's mostly coarse sand and artificial turf, with separate areas for small and large dogs. Note that at lunchtime on weekdays, it can be packed with dogs and professional dog walkers. There is a parking lot.

There are three other designated areas where dogs can be off-leash: between MLK Drive and Lincoln Way, near 5th Avenue; directly north of MLK Drive and Sunset Boulevard; and Kezar Triangle.

Key park rules for dog owners: Dogs should be leashed except in the areas listed above (dog owners can also read more about possible encounters with coyotes on p. 144). Immediately put a stop to digging and other destructive behavior. And of course, always pick up poop! Also note that dogs are prohibited in the Botanical Garden or Japanese Tea Garden except for service animals.

Food and Drink

Unlike the city as a whole, the park isn't a foodie's paradise. Depending on where you are and what day of the week it is, there may not be much of anything nearby. Weekends and summertime have more offerings, mostly on the eastern end of the park. Options have improved over time, but are still mostly standard fare with a few exceptions.

Coffee and Hot Chocolate

There are days when a hot beverage is crucial in the park (see Weather: Wind and Fog earlier). The **Flywheel Coffee** kiosk is on the far eastern edge of the park at 601 Stanyan Street next to the bocce courts. This is coffee for people who care about coffee (the main shop is across the street). **The Goldman Tennis Center** at Nancy Pelosi Drive and Bowling Green Drive has a vending machine inside that brews an affordable, decent cup of coffee or hot chocolate. There's free Wi-Fi here, too. **California Kahve** is next to the carousel. Closed Mondays and Tuesdays (except in the summer), they have espresso, coffee, and matcha, plus yummy treats, sandwiches, and smoothies.

The **coffee and pastry stand** behind the Bandshell on the Music Concourse is run by Annie's Hot Dogs and has a full espresso machine and range of drink options. On weekends, there's also often a coffee truck near the main entrance to the Botanical Garden on 9th Avenue. The **Blue Heron Boathouse** serves espresso, coffee, and hot chocolate. The **Golden Gate Park Golf Course Clubhouse** is at the far western end of the park. They have coffee, pastries, and some indoor seating. No need to use the golf course to enjoy the clubhouse.

Food Trucks and Stands

Most days you can count on an **Annie's Hot Dogs** stand set up at the corner where JFK Promenade hits Hagiwara Tea Garden Drive (at the northeastern corner of the Music Concourse) and behind the Bandshell. Annie's serves a range of hot dogs and sausages (including a vegan one), plus pretzels, ice cream, and drinks. On the weekends and holidays, Annie's Hot Dogs also usually pops up at Spreckels Lake, near the Conservatory of Flowers, and by the Botanical Garden's North Gate.

On weekends, you'll find a variety of **food trucks** parked behind the Bandshell on the Music Concourse, and usually on JFK Promenade. There's often an ice cream truck on weekend afternoons on MLK Drive near the Music Concourse.

Cafés and Restaurants

Every day except Mondays, the **de Young Museum's café** offers a more upscale (and pricey) menu ranging from salads and sandwiches to salmon and stews. The indoor seating is fine, but the outdoor seating on the Osher Sculpture Garden's terrace is really nice in the summer months (when they remove the tent) for a leisurely lunch. You don't have to pay museum admission to go to the café.

The **California Academy of Science's café** is open daily but only to ticket holders; the food is kid-friendly, somewhat overpriced fare. However, the Academy's **Terrace Restaurant** (also for ticket holders only) is better quality for similar prices, with some separation from the throngs of kids.

While seating is limited and can be hard to come by, the **Japanese Tea Garden's Tea House** is a charming option with "light snacks and sweet treats," including fortune cookies (which were invented here; read more on p. 76). The Tea House can get you by until a real meal; try the iced green tea. The open-air, covered seating is in the heart of the garden.

The **Blue Heron Boathouse café** offers a range of grilled burgers and sandwiches, salads, wraps, a kids' menu, and vegan wraps and sausages. The café also serves espresso drinks and beverages, including beer and wine. They describe their French fries as "famous"; I like their onion rings even better. There's some indoor

Surrounded by gardens and sculptures, the outdoor terrace at the de Young Museum is wonderful on a nice day. *(Photo by Jim Watkins)*

seating and plenty of picnic tables nearby. The kitchen opens at 11 a.m. daily, but closing hours vary depending on the season and day of week, so check their website at blueheronboathouse.com if you're considering going there after 4 p.m.

At the far western end of the park directly across the street from Ocean Beach, you'll find the **Beach Chalet Brewery and Restaurant**, plus **Park Chalet**—both at 1000 Great Highway. **Beach Chalet Brewery and Restaurant** is a higher-end establishment, where prices reflect the views of the Pacific from the second story. It's usually open every day, with some special offerings like champagne brunches and five-course dinners paired with local wines. Go to beachchalet.com for hours, special offerings, and live music schedules. The on-site brewery makes a nice range of beers that you can order at the restaurant or at Park Chalet.

Downstairs (without the views) is **Park Chalet**. Park Chalet offers an airy atrium of indoor seating, but it's known for its large outdoor seating area that feels like a beer garden on a nice day. Park Chalet offers good pub fare like fish and chips, burgers, and clam chowder. The outdoor seating often becomes packed with families on nice days, especially with people coming from the Beach Chalet Athletic Fields. Check parkchalet.com for hours, which vary by season, as well as happy hours and live music schedules.

There's one last far-west food option, which is the **Golden Gate Park Golf Course Clubhouse**. Open daily, the grill operates from 10 a.m. to 3:30 p.m., serving the original Hot Dog Bills Burgerdog and other food and drinks at reasonable prices—including baked goods and coffee. The patio is one of the best-kept secrets in the park. There's also free Wi-Fi here.

Food Options near the Park

More interesting and satisfying than most of the park's options are the countless bakeries, cafés, and restaurants in nearby neighborhoods: Haight-Ashbury, Cole Valley, Inner Sunset, Inner Richmond, Outer Sunset, and Central and Outer Richmond. But that might overwhelm you with possibilities! So if you're hungry, my recommendation is to focus on **Irving Street**, which runs a block off the southern border of the park and has almost every food imaginable on it, including plenty of affordable options.

The 9th and Irving area, plus the 19th and Irving area, have especially high concentrations of delicious options. The N Judah light rail is right there, too, so you can jump on to head west or east along the park (all the way to the ocean or downtown).

Picnicking

Picnicking can be as simple as bringing a sandwich and finding a bench, or as extravagant as some of the spreads I've seen at Opera in the Park, complete with crystal champagne glasses. On weekends, food trucks on JFK Promenade make an impromptu picnic easy.

You can picnic pretty much anywhere in the park. **The lawns around the Conservatory of Flowers** are picturesque, with nice grass, restrooms, and great people-watching on JFK Promenade. Windy? Go to nearby Peacock Meadow for less wind thanks to a stand of big trees. **14th Avenue East Meadow** and **Pioneer East Meadow** have plenty of space to spread out. **Hippie Hill**, an iconic hangout since the 1960s, is where you'll hear the sound of drums and pickleball games, and it's also where events with picnicking, like Opera in the Park, are held. It also has restrooms.

Lindley Meadow, Marx Meadow, and **Hellman Hollow** are found in the western half of the park; these are popular for large group picnics, thanks to tables, barbeque grills (at some tables), and wide-open spaces for activities. This stretch of JFK Drive allows private vehicles, so you can drive supplies relatively close to these areas to unload. For a romantic spot off JFK Drive, go to the small meadow on the far side of Lloyd Lake. **The Great Meadow at the Botanical Garden** is one of the best places to put down a blanket in the park, and this pastoral setting feels peaceful even on busy weekend days. Admission required. There are many tasty options for picking up food nearby around 9th and Irving.

I have a few favorite places to picnic off the beaten path. **The lawn area in the National AIDS Memorial Grove** is less windy and crowded (but the grass can be wet). The **Moon Viewing Garden** and **Conifer Lawn** are lovely, quieter spots in the **Botanical Garden**; note you can stay after the gates close. The **Shakespeare Garden** is small, quiet, and convenient to get to—a sweet place for a picnic date. **Metson Lake** is a charming area with a little waterfall and creek that kids love playing in. The lawn across the street (Middle Drive West) is perfect for a blanket and tossing a frisbee. This was John McLaren's favorite lake, and it's mine, too.

USING PICNIC TABLES IN THE PARK

There are picnic tables scattered throughout the park, and if they're empty, go for it! But note that most picnic areas can be reserved, and on the weekends, they often are. So if you want to plan a larger picnic and guarantee the use of certain picnic tables (some have barbeque grills), get a permit. Picnic areas can be reserved up to ninety days in advance, and fees start at around $50, depending on the size of your group. Learn more at sfrecpark.org.

Note that if you have a lot of supplies and plan to drive, you will need to transport your stuff on foot if the location is off of JFK Promenade, where no private vehicles are allowed. Also, beer and wine are generally allowed at picnic areas, but not hard liquor or kegs.

Want to host a larger, last-minute picnic? Just north of Bunny Meadow, close to the Conservatory of Flowers, is a first-come, first-served area—the Ghirardelli Card Shelter—with several picnic and game tables.

WHERE TO GET PICNIC SUPPLIES

If you're looking for a large grocery store for supplies and a spread of premade foods, there are **four major grocery stores near the park**. At the far eastern edge of the park, Whole Foods at 690 Stanyan Street is a frequent stop for picnickers. Very near the Music Concourse area is the Safeway at 735 7th Avenue. About a

The lawns near the Conservatory of Flowers are the most popular and classic picnic spot in the park. *(Photo by Jim Watkins)*

ten-minute walk from the main entrance of the Botanical Garden is Andronico's at 1200 Irving Street. And if you're at the far western end of the park, there's a Safeway at 850 La Playa Street. All of these stores offer hot food and salad bars plus paper plates, drinks, and utensils.

What to Do with One Day in the Park

This book is meant to help you discover and explore as many sides of the park as possible, ideally with plenty of time to do so. But sometimes all you get is one day! Most tourists, in part because of tour buses and attraction packages, head to the Music Concourse area when they're on a tighter schedule. That's perfectly fine. The Music Concourse is beautiful, and there's plenty to do right around there. You'll get a feel for the park and have a great time, plus everything is nearby and accessible for people with limited mobility.

But when possible, you should also experience some of the park's wildness, natural wonder, and good vibes. Here are some recommendations, all on the eastern half of the park, to maximize your time.

Walk or ride a bike along JFK Promenade. JFK Promenade is the "Main Street" and commons of the park. Starting at the far eastern end at McLaren Lodge, there are plenty of sights along the 1.5-mile stretch of car-free street going west. Even if you just walk on JFK Promenade from the Conservatory of Flowers to 8th Avenue, you'll experience the joy of this space. If mobility is an issue, sitting near the Conservatory of Flowers is a way to take in the scene; you can also ride the free shuttle along JFK Promenade for all or part of the way.

Five Official Things You'll Find in the Park

1. San Francisco's official flower: the dahlia
2. San Francisco's official Christmas tree: the Monterey cypress known as "Uncle John's Tree," next to McLaren Lodge
3. California's official flower: the golden poppy
4. California's official tree: the coastal redwood
5. America's official land mammal: the bison

If you have only one day in the park and are feeling overwhelmed, rest assured that you really can't go wrong. Just get out there! *(Photo by Jim Watkins)*

JFK Promenade also helps you get a sense of the scale of Golden Gate Park and San Francisco. The Promenade is half the length of the 3-mile-long park, which stretches almost halfway across the 7-by-7-mile city.

Go to a garden or two and a forest or few. The Botanical Garden or the Japanese Tea Garden are tops, but the quieter Dahlia Dell (formerly known as the Dahlia Garden), Fuchsia Dell, Rhododendron Dell, and Shakespeare Garden are also nice options. Then experience a redwood forest in the National AIDS Memorial Grove or Heroes Grove, or hike in the oak woodlands in the northeast corner of the park.

Take in a view if it's not foggy; take in something new if it is. On clear days, the 360-degree view from the Hamon Observation Tower (which is free) in the de Young Museum lets you see downtown, the Golden Gate Bridge, and the Pacific

Ocean. If you're feeling more ambitious, hike to the top of Strawberry Hill for a great vista.

If it's a gray day, pick one of the indoor major attractions on the Music Concourse instead and use this book for some insider tips. Rainy day? If you're dressed for the weather, go to the Japanese Tea Garden. Some parts are designed to gather and reflect the rain, and you can take it in without the crowds.

Do you have kids with you? Check out my tips for the California Academy of Sciences (see p. 58), consider adding a playground into your day (see p. 94), hunt for fairy doors (see p. 103), or do the monastery stones walk (see p. 178).

If you have only one day, should you do a private tour of the park? There are many paid guided tour options these days, including ones on Segways, bicycles, e-bikes, and on foot. While tour buses often have Golden Gate Park as a destination, they don't actually tour the park.

How do you most enjoy a new place? Do you have the time and want the flexibility to explore lesser-known locations? Are you able to walk or bike quite a bit? Answering these questions will help you decide if you want to do a tour of some kind or just hit the park with this book in hand.

If you're looking for a deeper knowledge of the park (if you're reading this book, you probably are), go to sfcityguides.org to see if there's a free expert-led tour that day in the park.

There are also self-guided audio tour options. KQED's *Bay Curious* podcast has an audio tour of Golden Gate Park with six roughly fifteen-minute episodes on the park's origins, the National AIDS Memorial Grove, the Japanese Tea Garden, the bison, the Dutch Windmill, and the Polo Field. Reporters and park-lovers Heather Knight and Peter Hartlaub take listeners on a ninety-minute tour of the park via the VoiceMap app; search for "Secrets of Golden Gate Park." A wide range of podcasts that go deep into the park's history can be found at outsidelands.org.

ATTRACTIONS, ENTERTAINMENT, AND ACTIVITIES

The park's major attractions offer something for everyone, from mind-expanding planetarium and art exhibits to close encounters with rare plants and animals from faraway places. All the attractions have their own stories that, once you know them, illuminate new dimensions of the park.

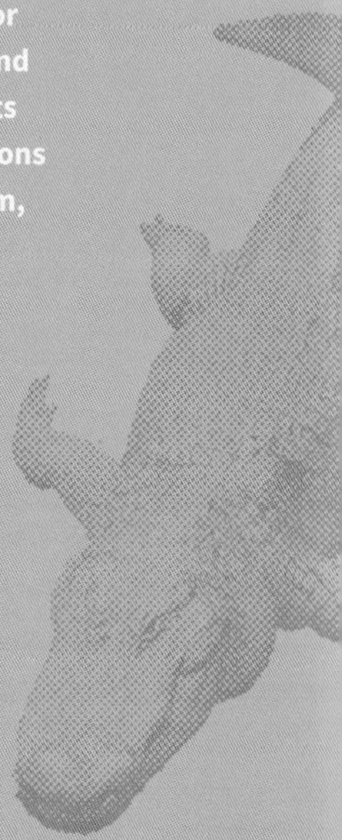

Opposite: *The tulips planted in the Queen Wilhelmina Garden bloom in March and April. (Photo by Jim Watkins)*

Museums and Attractions

Locals enjoy an embarrassment of riches within the park, with world-class museums and enchanting attractions.

Would it be so wrong to visit San Francisco and spend your entire time in Golden Gate Park? I would never judge you. Because once you read this section, you'll wonder what you're willing to miss.

The California Academy of Sciences

This spectacular science museum houses a coral reef, rainforest, planetarium, and more.	
	ADDRESS: 55 Music Concourse Drive
	PHONE: (415) 379-8000
	WEBSITE: calacademy.org
	HOURS: Open daily, 365 days a year. Weekend and holiday mornings are generally packed with kids. Weekday afternoons are the quietest time at the Academy. Hours vary by day of the week; members get early entry on certain days of the week.
	AMENITIES: The Academy Café and the Terrace Restaurant offer food; restrooms and gift shops are also available.

The California Academy of Sciences was founded in 1853 in San Francisco by a handful of curious men wanting to better understand all the plants, animals, and minerals of the western United States. It was started as a group rather than a museum, and the group grew quickly in membership, scope, and importance.

The Academy had corresponding members including famous biologist Charles Darwin and was ahead of its time in actively welcoming women. The Academy began collecting and displaying specimens in a space in downtown San Francisco, moving eventually to the six-story 833 Market Street building in 1890. This was the worst possible location for a new science museum given what was to come.

The 1906 earthquake—and the fires that swept through downtown afterward—destroyed the museum and almost all its contents. Incredibly, in the midst of the growing fires, Alice Eastwood, the director of botany for the Academy, raced to the Academy from her home in Nob Hill on a rescue mission. Despite the stairs having

The Academy includes the Osher Rainforest, which takes you from the forest canopy down four stories to an underwater view of a flooded Amazon forest. *(Photo by Jim Watkins)*

been destroyed by the quake, Eastwood climbed the metal banisters to the sixth floor of the Academy to rescue her "in case of emergency" collection of nearly 1,500 specimens. She lowered them out the window (with the help of a friend she'd run into on the way), climbed back down the banisters, and successfully saved the Academy's most valuable plant specimens and records.

After the dust settled, the Academy needed a new home to rebuild its collections in. Because it was far from where the fires had been, Golden Gate Park was considered a good option by many. Michael Henry de Young's *San Francisco Chronicle* heartily endorsed it, likely because it would bring more people to the de Young Museum (which was already in the park). Interestingly, park superintendent John McLaren welcomed the Academy despite generally wanting less development in the park. His friendship with Alice Eastwood may have played a role. Voters were on board, too, passing a measure to authorize the Academy to relocate to the park.

The Academy is home to two giant aquariums: a living Philippine coral reef and the California Coast shown here. *(Photo by Jim Watkins)*

The first Academy building in Golden Gate Park opened in 1916. Many more buildings and features were added over the years, like the Steinhart Aquarium in 1923 and the Morrison Planetarium in 1952. Eventually, there were twelve buildings making up the complex, and around 800,000 visitors a year.

After the 1989 Loma Prieta earthquake significantly damaged these older buildings, plans for a new era began. The state-of-the-art structure you see today was built between 2005 and 2008. The "new Academy" (as it's still known to some) includes some nods to the past. The front of the building includes two walls from what was—and still is—the African Hall. The inside of the African Hall was painstakingly recreated, with artists painting new versions of the murals to match the old ones, and taxidermists restoring the mounted animals to look more alive than ever.

The carved seahorse railings around the Swamp are replicas from the old Academy (with narrower spacing because kids used to get their heads stuck in the bars). The giant pendulum on the far side of the planetarium was also in the old Academy. And of course, the live animals came back—all 38,000 of them.

The beautiful, LEED-certified green building was designed by architect Renzo Piano, whose idea was to "lift up a piece of the park and put a building underneath." The two biggest domes on the **Living Roof** (which you can walk on) are the tops of the **Morrison Planetarium** and the **Osher Rainforest**.

The Academy continues to be a beloved attraction and destination science museum today. The 212,000-gallon aquarium with a living **Philippine coral reef** is spectacular—and so is the 100,000-gallon **California Coast** tank showing what the waters off San Francisco are like. You can feel a 7.9-magnitude earthquake (like the great 1906 San Francisco quake) in the **Shake House**. You can watch **flashlight fish** blink on and off. You can marvel at an actual **blue whale skeleton**, the largest creature ever to live on Earth. Or you can **go frogging** to search for the tomato frog, glass frog, and Panamanian golden frog. Additionally, the Academy holds a ticketed event for ages twenty-one and up called **NightLife** most Thursdays, with special activities, dancing, and drinks.

Beyond what you experience as a visitor, the Academy conducts groundbreaking research and conservation efforts. Its aquarium was the first in the United States to spawn baby corals. The Academy also keeps building its unbelievable collection of specimens from around the world: 46 million and counting (by the way, botanist Alice Eastwood is credited for an unbelievable 350,000 of these)!

Three Tips for When You Arrive

1. Sign up immediately for tickets to a **Morrison Planetarium show** in the lobby. These fill up quickly, even for afternoon screenings. Whatever is being shown in this immersive theater is usually worth seeing (note that these shows are only for kids four and up).

2. Check the schedule for the in-tank diver presentations in the Philippine coral reef tank, and then plan to get to the viewing area early for a good spot.

3. See how long the lines for the Shake House and the rainforest are, and jump in if they're reasonable.

Two particular animals at the Academy have gotten a lot of special press over the years. **Claude, the albino alligator,** came to the Academy in 2008. He's now a beloved mascot and possibly the world's most famous alligator, thanks to his lack of pigmentation. His "hatch day" is celebrated every September 15, and there's a charming children's book by local author Emma Bland Smith about him. Find Claude in the Swamp.

DNA analysis in 2023 proved that **Methuselah, the Australian lungfish,** is pushing one hundred years of age and is officially the world's oldest aquarium fish. She arrived at the Academy in 1938, likes belly rubs and fresh figs, and unlike most gilled fish can gulp air at the water surface. Find Methuselah as you head down the stairs to the aquarium level, across from the alligators.

Find These Five Fascinating Animals at the Academy

Over the years with my kids, I've developed my own list of must-see animals. If you visit all five of these charismatic creatures, it will take you to most parts of the Academy, with plenty to see along the way:

1 **Leafy seadragons.** These rare and surreal fish from Australia are a must-see in the round tank in the Water Planet area of the aquarium level.

2 **African penguins.** You can't go wrong with these cute and comical birds, which are endangered in the wild. Find these in the African Hall on the first floor.

3 **Stingrays.** Marvel at the range of stunning stingrays, like the honeycomb ray, gliding below you in the Reef Lagoon near the planetarium entrance on the first floor.

4 **Speckled sanddabs.** These super-camouflaged fish are supercool thanks to eyes that grow on just one side of their head, allowing them to lay on the seafloor. Their tank is tucked away on the aquarium level at the far end of the California Coast tank.

5 **Spotted garden eels.** Below the sharks and tropical fish, these eels play hide-and-seek from within the sand. Head to the Children's Eel Garden in the coral reef on the aquarium level.

Claude just might be the world's most famous alligator. If he's doing more than lazing around, consider yourself lucky! *(Photo by Jim Watkins)*

GETTING THERE

PUBLIC TRANSIT: The Academy is directly served by the 44 Muni bus line. The 5 and 5R Muni buses have stops at Fulton Street and 10th Avenue, a two-block walk to the Academy. The 7, N Judah, and 28 lines have stops with a ten- to fifteen-minute walk to the Academy. The free Golden Gate Park Shuttle also directly serves the Academy (see Transportation on p. 37).

BICYCLE: There is bicycle parking near the front entrance to the Academy, as well as in the underground parking lot.

DRIVING: There is a curbside drop-off zone in front of the Academy, which can be reached from the south side of the park, via MLK Drive. Navigate to Music Concourse Drive. Passengers can also be dropped off curbside inside the Music Concourse garage. This can be reached two ways: from the north side of the park via Fulton Street (at 10th Avenue) or from the south via MLK Drive to Music Concourse Drive. This garage is an eight-hundred-space paid parking lot under the Music Concourse, which is definitely the most secure place for your vehicle. This can fill up by the afternoon on busy days; if it's full, look for on-street parking on MLK Drive and other nearby park and neighborhood streets. Be advised to never leave valuables or *anything* interesting-looking inside your car. A free twenty-two-space ADA parking lot is right behind the Bandshell on the Music Concourse, about five hundred feet from the de Young Museum entrance. The underground Music Concourse parking garage has thirty-three paid ADA spaces.

ADMISSION: Free for members and children two and under. Ticket prices vary; there are small discounts for purchasing in advance. Purchasing online can also help you avoid long lines and guarantee against sold-out tickets. Note that tickets are pricey enough that you won't want to just spend an hour or so, and when it's crowded, you need time to even just hit the highlights.

Active-duty military personnel get a small discount every day; all veteran, retired, and active-duty military personnel get free admission on Veterans Day and during Fleet Week. There are also deeply discounted tickets for EBT/CalFresh, WIC, Lifeline Pass, and Medi-Cal cardholders.

For locals with some lead time, you can use your library card to access the "Discover & Go" program to get a free one-day Academy pass once a year. For tourists, some of the city passes include the Academy in their offerings, generally a good value given the ticket prices.

The Academy has a range of accessibility resources and policies for deaf, hearing-impaired, blind, or partially sighted guests. It also has sensory kits to check out and a sensory map showing where high levels of different types of sensory stimuli are in the Academy.

Tips for Bringing Very Young Kids to the Academy

The Academy is a wonderful, welcoming place for the under-five crowd. Here are five important things to know:

1. Parents are allowed to push a stroller, but doing so can be challenging with crowds. The policy and practice is to leave your stroller in an out-of-the-way spot. You can rent lockers in the lobby, but they aren't large enough for a stroller or luggage.

2. Check the daily schedule when you arrive. There is often a puppet show or other programs that are great for the under-five crowd.

3. Kids must be at least four years old to attend Planetarium shows. The Academy recommends seven and older. However, there are daily programs about space and the stars for little ones in Hohfeld Hall—no reservations required.

4. There is a designated space for nursing and an all-gender family restroom in the indoor Curiosity Grove play space, which is intended for kids five and under.

5. All restrooms have changing tables, and there's a family restroom by the Swamp.

The de Young Museum's twisting tower, with exceptional views, is free and open to the public. *(Photo by Jim Watkins)*

De Young Museum and the Hamon Observation Tower

This premier art museum has a wide range of collections, a 360-degree observation tower, and gardens.	
	ADDRESS: 50 Hagiwara Tea Garden Drive
	PHONE: (415) 750-3600
	WEBSITE: famsf.org
	HOURS: Open daily except Mondays; check the website for any holiday closures.
	AMENITIES: The museum has a café, restrooms (including one family restroom), and gift shops.

The de Young Museum is one of the top ten most visited art museums in the United States. It's home to American art from the seventeenth century through today, textile arts and costumes, African art, Oceanic art, arts of the Americas, and international contemporary art. It's such a diverse collection that you *will* find something you like, and have fun on the way (even with kids) because the building itself is so interesting. Special exhibits run the gamut from ancient Egyptian artifacts to haute couture. The docent-led "highlights tours," free with admission, are a great way to get acquainted with some of the museum's best offerings.

The history of the de Young Museum is almost as old as the park itself. In 1893, a complex of temporary buildings and pavilions was hastily built on 160 acres of parkland for the California Midwinter International Exposition of 1894. Local businessman Michael Henry de Young had spearheaded the idea of the exposition after being part of a similar one in Chicago. He thought it would boost the local economy (and probably his advertising revenues at the *San Francisco Chronicle*, the newspaper he had started with his brother).

De Young had been a collector since he was a child and thought a museum in the park was a good idea (he also wanted a place to put his stuff). So when the 1894 Midwinter Exposition ended and demolition began, de Young convinced the president of the park commission at the time to keep one of the buildings. The following year, this building became the Memorial Museum (to remember how great the Expo had been—seriously!) and initially was filled mostly with de Young's personal collection and items from the Expo. It was like an eclectic Smithsonian.

Later, de Young footed the bill for a huge expansion right next to the first building, complete with a tower. The expanded museum was then named in de Young's honor when it opened in 1921. De Young continued to find and purchase items for the museum, and he left a large bequest for it when he died in 1925. It was then that the museum transitioned to a fine art museum—and a world-class one at that.

In 1989, the Loma Prieta earthquake significantly damaged the museum and forced a reckoning about its future, including whether it should stay in the park versus move to a downtown location. Ultimately, what had become the M. H. de Young Museum *was* rebuilt in the same spot in the park and is now

Did You Know?

The pattern on the copper exterior of the de Young was based on photos of the sky filtering through the park's tree canopy. It took over a million embossings to create the look. Eventually the copper will turn green, but no one knows when.

known simply as "the de Young." It was designed by renowned Swiss architecture firm Herzog and de Meuron with a vision for intertwining museum visitors, art, and the park.

The twisting Hamon Observation Tower was somewhat controversial at the time for its height and modern style, but it was a nod to the museum's previous tower. The tower provides unparalleled views of the park and beyond from a 144-foot vantage point on the 9th floor. You can go for free during museum hours. When you go to the tower, be sure to check out the fifteen woven-wire sculptures by groundbreaking artist and activist Ruth Asawa, who selected this collection to donate to the museum. Asawa's famous sculptures hang from the ceiling near the elevators to the tower. Asawa's work was first exhibited at the de Young in 1960, when she began gaining recognition as an artist. Asawa lived in San Francisco for most of her life until her death in 2013. Her funeral was held outside the de Young on the Music Concourse, where she once drew the trees with her children.

Besides the tower and Ruth Asawa's sculptures, there are **a couple of other attractions in and around the de Young that don't require tickets.** At the front entrance of the museum, look for the very long crack in the paving and stones. This is *Drawn Stone*, by prominent large-scale nature-based artist Andy Goldsworthy, a

The long crack in the paving and stones leading up to the de Young is *Drawn Stone* by Andy Goldsworthy.

reminder of the earthquakes that have shaped the land and history of San Francisco and California. Also free are the two gardens on either end of the de Young. The **Marcus Garden of Enchantment** (open 24/7) includes sculptures from the museum's early days, plus modern surprises. The **Osher Sculpture Garden** (open during museum hours) has the don't-miss sculpture *Three Gems* by James Turrell, where you enter a "skyspace." Nearby is a sculpture called *Exomind* of a woman whose head is covered with an active beehive—for real—on view Thursday through Sunday and the first Tuesday of the month (but only if it's warm enough out, so not that often!).

GETTING THERE

PUBLIC TRANSIT: The de Young is directly served by the 44 Muni bus. The 5 and 5R Muni buses have stops at Fulton Street and 10th Avenue, a two-block walk to the de Young. The 7 and 28 Muni buses and the N Judah streetcar have stops with a ten- to fifteen-minute walk to the de Young. The free Golden Gate Park Shuttle also directly serves the de Young (see Transportation on p. 37).

BICYCLE: There is bicycle parking near all three entrances to the de Young, as well as in the underground parking lot.

DRIVING: There is a curbside drop-off zone in front of the de Young, which can be reached from the south side of the park via MLK Drive to Music Concourse Drive. Passengers can also be dropped off curbside inside the Music Concourse garage. This can be reached two ways: from the north side of the park via Fulton Street (at 10th Avenue) or from the south via MLK Drive to Music Concourse Drive. This garage is an eight-hundred-space paid parking lot under the Music Concourse, which is definitely the most secure place for your vehicle. This can fill up by the afternoon on busy days; if it's full, look for on-street parking on MLK Drive and other nearby park and neighborhood streets. Be advised to never leave valuables or anything interesting inside your car. A free twenty-two-space ADA lot is right behind the Bandshell on the Music Concourse, about five hundred feet from the de Young entrance. The underground Music Concourse parking garage has thirty-three paid ADA spaces.

ADMISSION: Free for members. Admission is required for the permanent collection galleries, with discounted rates for seniors and students. Kids ages seventeen and under enjoy free admission to the permanent collection every day. At 4:30 p.m. daily, *everyone* receives free admission to the permanent collection.

First Tuesdays of the month are free for all. Every Saturday, general admission is free for all residents of the nine Bay Area counties (reserve online). Some "all-in-one" tourist museum passes include the de Young. Special exhibits always require additional tickets and can sell out. Note that paid admission for the de Young is good on the same day for the Legion of Honor, which is about 2.5 miles away and features European art.

The Hamon Observation Tower within the de Young is *always* free to the public, and it's a must-do for a spectacular 360-degree view of the park. Much of the first floor is also open to the public and is worth a look to experience the architecture (and its nice bathrooms).

San Francisco Botanical Garden at Strybing Arboretum

This fifty-five-acre garden of gardens showcases California natives and redwoods alongside rare plants and trees from around the world.

ADDRESS: 1199 9th Avenue

PHONE: (415) 661-1316

WEBSITE: gggp.org

HOURS: Open daily at 7:30 a.m.; closing hours vary depending on the time of year. Note that you can stay an hour after the final entry, which is one of the best tips in this entire book!

AMENITIES: There are restrooms and a gift shop. The restroom nearest the North Gate is wheelchair accessible.

Whether or not you're "into plants," the fifty-five-acre Botanical Garden is worth visiting for its lush beauty, meandering paths, and peaceful vibes. You can practically feel your blood pressure go down as you take in the sheer variety of flowers and foliage. San Francisco's climate makes it conducive to growing plants from around the world, including remote locations with some very unique plants and trees from the cloud forests of Central America, South America, and Southeast Asia, which thrive here, as well as rare high-elevation palms and plants from New Zealand and Asia. The garden has become a refuge for endangered plants threatened by deforestation and climate change.

Volunteer docents lead 1- to 1.5-hour tours at 10:30 a.m. and/or 1 p.m. several times a week. If you definitely want to go on a tour, check ahead for dates and times for guided walks at gggp.org. The Botanical Garden has a tool called

"Garden Explorer" where you can search for any plant and get its precise location at sfbg.gardenexplorer.org. But wandering here is the way to go; give yourself at least an hour to explore.

No matter what time of year you visit, you'll find flowering plants. But the standout season might be mid-January through March, when the magnolias bloom. The garden boasts one of the most diverse and rare collections in the world. April and May will bring impressive displays of rhododendrons and California wildflowers, and the South Africa garden is spectacular. Fall brings out all kinds of colors and surprises in the various cloud forest gardens.

The garden is a birding hotspot, and there are free guided bird-watching walks on the first Sunday of the month (more on p. 136). Trees are, of course, a big part of the attraction for the birds. Some of the garden's trees are more than a century old, thanks to John McLaren. He got the idea for an arboretum in the late 1890s and started planting a variety of trees. The garden really got going in the 1930s, thanks to a large donation by Helene Strybing in honor of her husband. The Botanical Garden officially opened in 1940. (It used to be called Strybing

Tip: You can stay at the Botanical Garden after the gates close and enjoy this stunning part of the park in solitude. *(Photo by Jim Watkins)*

The Botanical Garden becomes an al fresco concert hall each year during Flower Piano. *(Photo by Jim Watkins)*

Arboretum, but it is now officially the San Francisco Botanical Garden at Strybing Arboretum.) Speaking of old trees, the Great Meadow is home to a Monterey cypress measuring at least one hundred feet tall that is likely a McLaren original. It's rather poetic that when legendary conservationist Jane Goodall visited the garden in 2024 right before her ninetieth birthday, she laid her hand on the tree. You can, too!

The garden's biggest event of the year (and one of the best events ever, anywhere) is Flower Piano, which features scheduled performances on multiple pianos scattered throughout the grounds. You can also play on any open pianos. Flower Piano is free with admission, except for some special concerts. Members enjoy a separate, expedited entry. The garden also hosts a range of events year-round like yoga, sketching, gardening, birding, and more. Visit gggp.org for a schedule.

The **Helen Crocker Russell Library of Horticulture** at the Botanical Garden is an incredible resource for gardeners and educators, and it has an extensive children's library. It also hosts art exhibits and children's story times, plus it's a good place to read some nature-themed picture books and take a breather. Check gggp.org for a schedule.

You will find many medieval monastery stones in the Botanical Garden (see p. 180 for more about the stones). The area to the left after you go through the main entrance is full of them, as are the Succulent Garden and Rhododendron Garden.

If you're visiting in March through June, be sure to go to the **California Native Garden** to see the pipevine swallowtails, both as large black caterpillars and as butterflies (look near the fence that runs along the pond).

Note that tree climbing in all areas is prohibited to protect the specimens. This is one of the few outdoor spaces in the park where dogs (except service animals) are not allowed. Bicycles and scooters are also prohibited, though you can walk your bike or scooter through to the other entrance/exit. There is bike parking near both entrances.

GETTING THERE

The Botanical Garden has two entrances: the Main Gate at 1199 9th Avenue, and the Friend (North) Gate near the intersection of MLK Drive and Hagiwara Tea Garden Drive. The Friend (North) Gate is very close to the Japanese Tea Garden; use the directions in Getting There for the Japanese Tea Garden if you want to arrive and enter there. The Main Gate is recommended for first-time visitors.

PUBLIC TRANSIT: The 7 and 43 Muni buses have stops at 9th Avenue and Lincoln Boulevard, less than a block from the Main Gate of the Botanical Garden. The

The Gardens of Golden Gate Park

In 2022, the Botanical Garden, the Japanese Tea Garden, and the Conservatory of Flowers merged into the **Gardens of Golden Gate Park**. Given the number of gardens in the park, this merger is confusing even to locals. What it means is if you purchase daily admission at any one of these attractions, your admission is good at all three that same day. San Francisco residents enjoy free admission to all three attractions every day with proof of residency. Note that there are certain times and days when anyone can enter for free—read more in the detailed section for each.

The Gardens of Golden Gate Park are the only gardens with admission in the park. All the other gardens are open to the public all the time, with two exceptions. The **CommUNITY Garden** next to Kezar Stadium is behind a locked gate. This garden, opened in 2013, has raised garden beds for locals to use and a native plant nursery. The other exception is the **community garden at the Golden Gate Park Senior Center**.

The Botanical Garden has one of the most diverse collections of magnolias in the world, and they're in full bloom January through March. *(Photo by Emily Rosenberg)*

N Judah streetcar has a stop 0.2 mile away from the Main Gate at 9th Avenue and Irving Street. The free Golden Gate Park Shuttle has a stop at the Japanese Tea Garden and the de Young Museum, which is very close to the Friend (North) Gate entrance (see Transportation on p. 37). The shuttle's California Academy of Sciences stop is 0.2 mile away from the Main Gate.

BICYCLE: Bicycle parking is near the Main Gate, and there are many more racks in front of the San Francisco County Fair Building next door. There is a small amount of bicycle parking near the Friend (North) Gate, plus many more racks behind the nearby Music Concourse.

DRIVING: There is a curbside drop-off zone at both the Main Gate and the Friend (North) Gate. Note that on weekends, 9th Avenue and MLK Drive can be very congested; you may want to be dropped off farther to the east in the park and then walk to one of the gates. There is free on-street parking along MLK Drive and Nancy Pelosi Drive; this fills up early on weekends. The Music Concourse garage is just 0.2 mile away (more on p. 42). This area has significant traffic on weekends; avoid driving

Five Favorites for Families at the Botanical Garden

During the pandemic, it felt like families finally discovered what I had known for years: the Botanical Garden is *great* with kids. Here are some of my kids' favorites:

1. **Temperate Asia.** This is where you'll find the bamboo forest (a must!), plus small ponds, bridges, and paths to explore.

2. **Ancient Plant Garden.** Search for the footprints of the hadrosaur, a plant-eating dinosaur, as you travel three hundred million years back in time through different periods of plant evolution.

3. **Redwood Grove.** This area, with its soft paths and towering trees, feels enchanted.

4. **The Children's Garden.** It's a bit of a hike to get to this part of the Botanical Garden (and a bit hard to find), but on Bean Sprouts Family Days, it's worth it. There are hands-on activities and supplies for digging, planting, and creating. See gggp.org for upcoming Family Days.

if you can. There are ADA spaces near both the Main Gate and the Friend (North) Gate , plus the free ADA lot in the Music Concourse 0.2 mile away.

ADMISSION: Admission can be purchased at the gate. There's no need to purchase tickets ahead of time online, though you can. Admission is also good that same day for the two other Gardens of Golden Gate Park: the Japanese Tea Garden and the Conservatory of Flowers. There is also a three-day pass to all three gardens available at gggp.org/tickets or in person at the Botanical Garden.

Free for Gardens of Golden Gate Park members, San Francisco residents with proof of residency, children ages four and under, military veterans, and those eligible for reduced admission with Museums for All. Free for all visitors on the second Tuesday of each month; daily from 7:30 a.m. to 9 a.m.; and on Thanksgiving, Christmas Day, and New Year's Day.

With so many hidden ponds, paths, bridges, and waterfalls, exploring the Botanical Garden with kids becomes an adventure for all ages.

5 **Monastery Stone Scavenger Hunt.** The Botanical Garden has hundreds of these carved medieval stones (see p. 180 for more information about the scavenger hunt, plus a map of the Botanical Garden).

Japanese Tea Garden and Tea House

The oldest public Japanese garden in the country has a five-story pagoda, drum bridge, and koi ponds.	ADDRESS: 75 Hagiwara Tea Garden Drive
	PHONE: (415) 752-1171
	WEBSITE: gggp.org/japanese-tea-garden
	HOURS: Open 365 days per year. The Japanese Tea Garden opens at 9 a.m. daily. From March through October the last entry is 5:30 p.m., and from November through February the last entry is 4:30 p.m.
	AMENITIES: Restrooms and a gift shop are available. The Tea House offers a variety of Japanese food and drink.

The Japanese Tea Garden is a beloved and popular destination in the park, often with long entry lines out front in the summer. But even when it's crowded, this garden has a tranquility to it, thanks to impeccable design and immaculate care. The Tea Garden is extra colorful during the cherry blossom season in March and April, but May brings wisteria, azaleas, rhododendrons, and irises. You can also take in fall foliage at the Tea Garden, thanks to the numerous Japanese maple and ginkgo trees.

The Tea Garden goes back to 1893, when a smaller version called the Japanese Village and Tea House was built as an attraction for the California Midwinter International Exposition, held in Golden Gate Park in 1894. It proved very popular, and unlike most of the Expo's attractions and structures, it got the green light to stay. Makoto Hagiwara, a talented landscape architect who had immigrated from Japan in 1878, was then hired to oversee the garden. He did this exceptionally well until 1900. That's when a new, anti-Asian city law meant to protect jobs for white workers forced Hagiwara out of his position.

By 1907, John McLaren was able to get the Tea Garden back into Hagiwara's capable hands and back in shape. McLaren, who was a friend of Hagiwara's, invited Hagiwara and his family to move to the garden, too. In 1910, Hagiwara built a house for his family, who joined him in expanding and enhancing the gardens. He also helped Japanese immigrants get started in San Francisco, exchanging room and board for some extra help on the grounds. In 1914, Hagiwara also made culinary history by inventing the modern fortune cookie for the Tea House. His sweeter take

The Japanese Tea Garden gets even lovelier during cherry blossom season in March and April. *(Photo by Jim Watkins)*

on a Japanese fortune cookie became very popular and in an only-in-America twist, is now served at Chinese restaurants all across the world—go figure! You can buy a small bag of fortune cookies in the gift shop.

The Tea Garden is just the right size to explore all of its paths within its five or so acres in about an hour. There are free, fascinating one-hour tours led by San Francisco City Guides at varying times daily. Find a schedule at sfcityguides.org. Note that, generally, the Japanese Tea Garden is *not* easy to navigate with a wheelchair or stroller, and dogs are prohibited (except service animals). If you need to stow a stroller, ask the folks at the front kiosk for help.

Meanwhile, after San Francisco hosted the 1915 Panama-Pacific International Exposition in what is now the Marina District, John McLaren moved the five-story pagoda and temple gates created for it to the Tea Garden. Visitors can now enjoy carefully restored versions of the pagoda and gates. (Listen for the bells in the pagoda when it is windy—which is most days.) Hagiwara died in 1925, and his family continued his legacy until the start of World War II, which sparked widespread racist, anti-Japanese hysteria in America. Japanese Americans throughout the West Coast were forced into internment camps, losing their property and livelihoods. In 1942, the Hagiwaras were sent to a camp, and their home was destroyed. Any mention of "Japan" was scrubbed from the Tea Garden, which was renamed the "Oriental Tea Garden."

It wasn't until 1952, nine years after John McLaren's death, that the word "Japanese" was put back in the Tea Garden's name. In 1974, a monument to the Hagiwara family, created by Japanese American artist Ruth Asawa, was placed

Listen for the bells in the five-story pagoda, which dates back to 1915. *(Photo by Jim Watkins)*

in the garden directly to the left after you enter. In 1985, the road in front of this area was renamed Hagiwara Tea Garden Drive. In recent years, this shameful but crucial piece of history has been more widely seen and shared, including in the media.

Today, the Tea Garden showcases exquisite Japanese-style horticulture and landscape design, much of it influenced by Buddhism, Shintoism, and Taoism. Every detail is intentional, bringing focus to nature's importance and our connection to it. The Dry Landscape Garden (a.k.a. the Zen Garden) uses stones and gravel to imply water features and landforms. Every path in the garden takes you on a miniature scenic adventure where you are meant to occasionally turn around to look at the view behind you as well.

Five Fun Tea Garden Activities with Kids

The Japanese Tea Garden has a special appeal for young kids, with many plants and pathways scaled to their size. Here's a checklist of things to do with little ones:

1. Find three frog sculptures made by Ruth Asawa. These are near the Main Gate on your way to the drum bridge.
2. Climb the drum bridge—a Tea Garden must!
3. Find and cross all four stone-step bridges. They are made with monastery stones (more on p. 178).
4. Find the good luck turtle carved into the boat-shaped granite water basin (*chōzubachi*) near the gift shop.
5. Search for the deer statue in the Maple Lane garden, and the crane statue in the Main Pond.

GETTING THERE

PUBLIC TRANSIT: The Tea Garden is directly served by the 44 Muni bus. The 5 and 5R Muni buses have stops at Fulton Street and 10th Avenue, a two-block walk to the Japanese Tea Garden. The 7, 28, and 28R Muni buses and the N Judah streetcar have stops with a ten- to fifteen-minute walk to the Tea Garden. The free Golden Gate Park Shuttle also directly serves the Tea Garden (see Transportation on p. 37).

BICYCLE: There is abundant bicycle parking behind the Music Concourse across the street, as well as between the entrance of the Tea Garden and the de Young Museum. There are also bike racks in the underground parking lot.

DRIVING: There is a curbside drop-off zone between the Tea Garden and the de Young Museum, which can be reached from the south side of the park via MLK Drive to Music Concourse Drive. There is an eight-hundred-space paid parking lot under the Music Concourse, which is definitely the most secure place for your vehicle. This can fill up by the afternoon on busy days; if it's full, look for on-street parking on MLK Drive and other nearby park and neighborhood streets. Be advised to never leave valuables or *anything* interesting inside your car. There is a free twenty-two-space ADA lot right behind the Bandshell on the Music Concourse, about a hundred feet from the Tea Garden entrance. The underground Music Concourse parking garage has thirty-three paid ADA spaces.

ADMISSION: Admission can be purchased at the gate. There's no need to purchase tickets ahead of time online. Admission is also good that same day for the two other Gardens of Golden Gate Park: the Conservatory of Flowers and the Botanical Garden. There is also a three-day pass to all three gardens available at gggp.org/tickets or in person at the Japanese Tea Garden.

Free for Gardens of Golden Gate Park members, San Francisco residents with proof of residency, children ages four and under, military veterans, and those eligible for reduced admission with Museums for All. Free for all visitors on Mondays, Wednesdays, and Fridays before 10 a.m.

The Survivor Trees

Near the pagoda in the Japanese Garden are a pair of ginkgo trees. They are called "survivor trees" (*hibakujumoku*) because they are descendants of trees that survived the atomic bomb that the United States dropped on Hiroshima, Japan, on August 6, 1945, during World War II, which killed more than 100,000 people.

These trees are a living connection to what happened both in Hiroshima and Nagasaki, where the United States dropped a second atomic bomb a few days later, on August 9, 1945. Survivor trees are being planted in cities around the world as a message of peace as part of the Green Legacy Hiroshima project.

To find these trees, go to the pavilion with the two large pagodas. On the eastern edge of the pavilion, you'll find a small Buddha statue. Look nearby (in the direction of the Tea House) for the two small ginkgo trees.

Ever since it opened in 1879, the Conservatory of Flowers has been quite popular as a background for photos. It is the oldest structure still standing in the park. *(Photo courtesy of Greg Gaar)*

Conservatory of Flowers

This iconic Victorian building is packed with 2,000 weird and wonderful plants.	
	ADDRESS: 100 JFK Drive
	PHONE: (415) 831-2090
	WEBSITE: gggp.org/conservatory-of-flowers
	HOURS: The Conservatory is closed on Wednesdays. It's open Thursday through Tuesday from 10 a.m. to 4:30 p.m., but the last entry is at 4 p.m.
	AMENITIES: The closest public restrooms are in a small building a short walk to the west. The Conservatory sells a small selection of gifts and plants.

The Conservatory of Flowers was one of the park's very first attractions and has certainly proven to be the most enduring. When you step inside America's oldest glass-and-wood greenhouse, it's not so different from when it first opened in 1879. Historical photos show that the giant water lily exhibit, for example, is almost exactly the same—and still a crowd-pleaser today (if you catch these in bloom, consider yourself very lucky).

Many park visitors don't realize that you can go inside the oldest glass-and-wood greenhouse in the country. *(Photo by Jim Watkins)*

The Conservatory is a living plant museum, so just like in an art museum, please look but don't touch. Over the years, the plants have gotten bigger and the collections more impressive. For example, an imperial philodendron called "Phil" hits the ceiling of the Conservatory and is more than a hundred years old, with six-foot-long leaves! The renowned orchid collection includes more than 700 of the existing 1,000 species, many from the remotest parts of the world, including an incredible range of *Dracula* orchids. The carnivorous pitcher plants—a favorite of all ages—are also plentiful and include some with fangs. The Conservatory is home to many plants that are highly endangered due to habitat destruction. Some are even considered extinct in the wild, like the golden fuchsia. You can also look for the plants that produce vanilla, cacao, and cinnamon to see the source of these all-time favorite flavors.

Any time of year, you'll enjoy the smells and faces of fantastical flowers, thanks to the careful curation of the Conservatory. Behind the main Conservatory are the greenhouses where plants hang out when they're not in bloom or put on display, which varies from month to month. The greenhouses contain several corpse flowers, which take years to store up enough energy to create a super-sized, super-stinky bloom for a few days. When a corpse flower blooms, it becomes a minor media sensation. Take a whiff if you have the chance—and, by the way, kids *love* this. They also like searching for the spooky-looking bat plant.

The Conservatory could easily not be standing today. A fire in 1883 took out the dome, which had to be rebuilt (and they made it even higher). Amazingly, the 1906 earthquake left the Conservatory fairly unscathed. But in December of 1995, a storm with 100-mile-per-hour winds shattered half of the 60,000 panes of glass. The estimated cost to repair the Conservatory was significant, and the possibility of tearing it down was all too real. But in 1998, First Lady Hillary Clinton took on the cause, raising the alarm bells for what she called a "national treasure" (and designated historical landmark). The attention helped to raise the $25 million needed, and the Conservatory reopened in 2003.

Note that the walkways inside the Conservatory are narrow. There's an area outside to put strollers. There's also an area inside the far western wing with small tables and chairs to sit and relax. There are no regular tours offered; however, if you see a volunteer, know that they're friendly and eager to share highlights. There is a self-guided audio tour available for a small fee through the CloudGuide app. Bring headphones if you plan to do this. There are occasional ticketed events like after-hours yoga and sound baths; check the calendar at gggp.org.

The Conservatory of Flowers has always been the most iconic backdrop within the park, with the postcards to prove it. It was also the backdrop for one of the 1906 earthquake refugee camps that were built in the park (more on p. 21). Since JFK Promenade was made car-free in 2020, the Conservatory's lawn has only further cemented its place as the park's "commons." The public piano on top of the Conservatory tunnel sometimes becomes an impromptu concert venue, and musicians often play on the opposite side of the tunnel from the Conservatory—those tunnel

The Breast Cancer Memorial Garden

Located northeast of the Conservatory of Flowers, where Arguello Boulevard and Conservatory Drives East and West meet

On the hill above the Conservatory of Flowers is the nation's first permanent public breast cancer memorial, completed in 2025. The garden offers benches and a peaceful, designated space for reflection and a view across the park to Sutro Tower. The memorial was created by Bay Area Young Survivors.

acoustics are excellent. There is usually a food truck nearby on weekends. In the immediate area of the Conservatory are two gardens to check out: the Dahlia Dell and the Breast Cancer Memorial Garden. And since 2017, an animated light show is projected nightly onto the sides of the Conservatory after dusk. It's worth bringing a blanket to sit and enjoy this unique show, which changes with the seasons. As for the flower beds around the Conservatory, they are replanted in spring and fall each year, with the most spectacular displays in the summer.

GETTING THERE

PUBLIC TRANSIT: The 5, 5R, and 33 Muni buses have stops at Fulton Street and Arguello Boulevard, a one-block walk (up a large hill) to the Conservatory. The free Golden Gate Park Shuttle also directly serves the Conservatory, with a stop at the intersection of JFK Promenade and Nancy Pelosi Drive (see Transportation on p. 37).

BICYCLE: There is bicycle parking near the restrooms next to the Conservatory.

DRIVING: There is a curbside drop-off zone behind the Conservatory that can be reached via Arguello Boulevard at Fulton Street. Two other good drop-off

The Dahlia Dell

Located just east of the Conservatory of Flowers at Pompei Circle off JFK Promenade

The Dahlia Dell is a must-see garden featuring San Francisco's official flower. Dahlias were given this lofty designation in 1926 because, thanks to their beauty and diversity, they are the "very symbol of San Francisco life and of the spirit of her people."

Dahlias, which are found wild in Mexico and Central and South America, can be hybridized into almost every possible color and color combination, plus a range of shapes, sizes, and forms. This leads to some truly exceptional blooms. The Dahlia Dell, formerly known as the Dahlia Garden, is known for hybridization innovation and boasts over seven hundred named hybrids. The garden's beauty is all thanks to volunteers, who have grown dahlias in this part of the park since the 1920s (except when the space was used for victory gardens during World War II). You can support their work and/or volunteer yourself through the Dahlia Society of California at dahliadell.org.

The Dahlia Society also hosts a flower show each August in the park, where gardeners across the state compete for the best blooms and sell a variety of dahlias. They also hold a plant and

locations are in front of the Goldman Tennis Center or McLaren Lodge. There is limited on-street parking on Fulton Street; better options include other parking lots or the Music Concourse garage (more on p. 42). There are ADA spaces on Nancy Pelosi Drive past the Goldman Tennis Center, across JFK Promenade from the Conservatory of Flowers.

ADMISSION: Admission can be purchased inside. There's no need to purchase tickets ahead of time online. Admission is also good that same day for the two other Gardens of Golden Gate Park: the Japanese Tea Garden and the Botanical Garden. There is also a three-day pass to all three gardens available at gggp.org/tickets or in person at the Conservatory.

Free for all visitors on the first Tuesday of the month. Free every day for Gardens of Golden Gate Park members, San Francisco residents with proof of residency, children ages four and under, military veterans, and those eligible for reduced admission with Museums for All.

tuber sale yearly in April and host occasional tours of the Dahlia Dell.

While you're at the dell, read the dahlia names, some of which are for local notables like Robin Williams. If you see a dahlia with a number, that's because it's a new hybridization. If the hybrid holds its form for three years and wins an award, the person who created it gets to name it. "Skip to My Lou" is a fan favorite, created by Lou Paradise, a renowned hybridizer. Don't miss the hillside garden while you're here; look for the stone shaped like California in the wall at the base. The garden blooms from May through November, with peak blooms July through September and the absolute peak in late August with more than 700 varieties.

Dahlias were made San Francisco's official flower in 1926 because they are the "very symbol of San Francisco life and of the spirit of her people." *(Photo by Jim Watkins)*

The National AIDS Memorial Grove

This ten-acre valley with memorials for those who died of AIDS is one of the most stunning parts of the park.	
	ADDRESS: Nancy Pelosi Drive and Bowling Green Drive, near the Goldman Tennis Center
	WEBSITE: aidsmemorial.org
	HOURS: Open during park hours from 5 a.m. to midnight.
	AMENITIES: The closest public restroom is at the Goldman Tennis Center.

If you talk with a San Franciscan who lived in the city during the AIDS epidemic, you will get a sobering window into the devastation experienced here at that time, especially in the gay community. *So many people* were dying of AIDS: more than 15,000 San Franciscans between 1981 and 1994.

In the late 1980s, an idea took root to have a designated space to grieve and remember loved ones lost to AIDS. This idea would eventually grow into a deeply moving and profoundly beautiful memorial.

The park offered up a 7.5-acre area that at the time was an overgrown, swampy dumping ground called de Laveaga Dell. It took volunteers three years to clean it up. But the hidden beauty of the valley began to reveal itself in the existing redwood trees, ravine, and defunct artificial creek. Volunteer architects and landscape designers, plus countless others, did the work to lovingly create what would become, in 1996, America's first and only designated memorial for those who died of AIDS. More than half a million Americans died of AIDS between 1982 and 2002.

Many people don't notice the National AIDS Memorial Grove, which is easy to miss despite now being ten acres and on the eastern end of the park. Others may not think it's for them because they don't have a personal connection to AIDS. But don't miss this part of the park—everyone is welcome here. The majority of the grove is wheelchair accessible, too.

Starting at the far eastern end, where most people enter the grove, you'll find the "Circle of Friends": a large, stone plaza engraved with the names of more than 3,500 people who died from AIDS. This is generally the most contemplative part of the grove; be mindful of others who may appreciate quiet. The Circle of Friends leads down into a small redwood forest with a creekbed made of smooth stones. After that, you'll cross a long lawn that's great for picnicking because the sunken valley is protected from the wind (bring a blanket for wet grass, though). At the far end of the valley, stairs lead up into soft paths next to a forested creek (one of my favorite places in the entire park), with a circular plaza and waterfall at the top. Continue above that to a smaller circular plaza. Here you can ring a large chime to remember the loved ones who were lost. To learn more about the grove's story, look up a piece by Barry R. Owen titled "San Francisco's Secret Paradise."

GETTING THERE

PUBLIC TRANSIT: The 7 Muni bus has a stop a few blocks away at Frederick Street and Arguello Boulevard. The N Judah streetcar has a stop about half a mile away at 2nd Avenue and Irving Street. The free Golden Gate Park Shuttle stops at the Goldman Tennis Center, which is across the street from the entrance to the National AIDS Memorial Grove.

Be sure to explore in and around the National AIDS Memorial Grove. This beautiful and secluded part of the park is often missed. *(Photo by Jim Watkins)*

BICYCLE: There is bicycle parking at the entrance, at the Goldman Tennis Center, and near the Lawn Bowling Club.

DRIVING: There is a curbside drop-off zone on Nancy Pelosi Drive near the corner of Bowling Green Drive. There is limited free on-street parking along Nancy Pelosi Drive and Bowling Green Drive. Be advised to never leave valuables or *anything* interesting-looking inside your car. There is just one ADA parking space right at the entrance, but there are several in front of the Goldman Tennis Center, a few hundred feet away, and in the parking lot at the Lawn Bowling Club, one block away.

JFK Promenade

This joyful stretch of park road is for people to stroll, roll, and enjoy art and nature—without any vehicle traffic!

ADDRESS: JFK Promenade, from Kezar Drive to Transverse Drive

HOURS: Open during park hours from 5 a.m. to midnight.

AMENITIES: There are public restrooms at multiple locations along JFK Promenade: McLaren Lodge, the Goldman Tennis Center, next to the Conservatory of Flowers, in the de Young Museum, and at the 14th Avenue East Meadow.

I often call JFK Promenade the happiest place in San Francisco. Thanks to activists, city leaders, and San Francisco voters, the park has 1.5 miles of car-free space on its main street. Made permanent and renamed JFK Promenade in 2022 (learn more in the Hero of the Park sidebar below), this is the most popular attraction in the park—and the number one most visited park space in the city. There are 200,000 visits on average each month!

JFK Promenade, which goes from the far eastern edge of the park to Transverse Drive, offers parkgoers a needed respite from vehicle traffic. But more than that, it's turned this part of the park into a true commons for the city: a giant, open-air living room. Whether you're a local or a tourist, everyone is part of the JFK Promenade community. Art installations, community pianos, and yellow Adirondack chairs all along JFK Promenade are thanks to local nonprofit Illuminate. Don't be shy: these are for you to enjoy. The "Love Blocks" sculptures on the lawn of the Conservatory and the submerged wooden whale next to the 14th Avenue East Meadow have become beloved features along JFK Promenade. Learn more at goldenmileproject.org.

The 1.5-miles of car-free space now called JFK Promenade has become one of the most popular park attractions. *(Photo by Jim Watkins)*

For people who never experienced JFK Promenade with traffic, it can be hard to imagine what it was like. I remember it well. Traffic—and there was plenty of it, including a lot of drivers simply cutting through the park—made this part of the park feel very different. But now, sitting on the lawn next to the Conservatory of Flowers, you can hear voices, laughter, and music instead of motors. Instead of the other side of the street being blocked by parked cars and trucks, it's one unified space to take in. You can relax, smile at strangers, and smell the fresh air, just like John McLaren intended. Even if you can't walk or ride a bike on JFK Promenade, find a bench or Adirondack chair to people-watch. The Golden Gate Park Shuttle runs seven days a week to help people get to and around JFK Promenade.

GETTING THERE

The free Golden Gate Park Shuttle has stops along JFK Promenade and connects directly with multiple transit stops and the ADA parking lot behind the Bandshell on the Music Concourse (more on p. 63).

Blue Heron Lake and the Boathouse

Waterfalls, historical bridges, boat rentals, and the highest point in the park are found here.

ADDRESS: 50 Blue Heron Lake Drive

WEBSITE: blueheronboathouse.com

HOURS: 10 a.m. to 5 p.m. daily

AMENITIES: The Blue Heron Boathouse has a café that opens at 11 a.m. daily, but closing times vary; check the website. It also has a souvenir shop. There is a public restroom behind the boathouse, across the small parking lot.

A Hero of the Park: David Miles Jr.

On April 2, 1967, 1.5 miles of JFK Drive were first closed to vehicle traffic and opened up for people to enjoy on Sundays and holidays. This development was thanks to City Supervisor Jack Morrison, who also cast the tie-breaking vote to prevent an eight-lane freeway from being built in the Panhandle (more on p. 24). The car-free space was an immediate hit and would continue on Sundays and holidays for more than fifty years. But over the years, as traffic in the park grew, it was increasingly apparent to some, including David Miles Jr., that a safe, car-free space in the park should exist *every day*. Miles, whose organizing had kept roller-skating from being banned in the park (more on p. 124), became a champion for this idea, with the San Francisco Bicycle Coalition joining Miles over the decades. Eventually, a small section of JFK Drive was also closed to vehicles on Saturdays for part of the year, starting in 2007.

Then the global pandemic happened in 2020. A local nonprofit, Walk San Francisco (my day job!), launched a campaign urging San Francisco's mayor at the time, London Breed, to close 1.5 miles of JFK Drive to traffic to create a

Blue Heron Lake (formerly known as Stow Lake) was created in 1893, turning Strawberry Hill into an island and creating two other small islands. Two bridges that cross the water to Strawberry Hill—Rustic Bridge and the Roman Bridge—were built at the same time. It was all completed just in time for the 1894 California Midwinter International Exposition. John McLaren's inspired design for Huntington Falls to cascade down Strawberry Hill was also completed the same year.

Blue Heron Lake was quickly the place for Victorian ladies with parasols to be paddled around in boats. Today, you can rent pedal and rowboats. Boating around the lake is a lot of fun and makes for a great date or family outing. Pedal boats fit up to four people, and rowboats fit up to three. Boats are rented by the hour and must be rented by 4 p.m. It's first-come, first-served, and there can be a wait on weekends, but it's worth checking to see how long the line is. Tip: If you have no boat preference, the rowboats are cheaper and the wait is shorter.

Enjoying Blue Heron Lake can be as simple as walking around the 1-mile loop on the outermost pedestrian path, which is fully accessible. But if you can, explore Strawberry Hill's interior paths along the water (a half-mile loop), especially around

safe space for people to be active while social distancing. On April 28, 2020, Mayor Breed used emergency powers to do just that. The car-free space quickly became very popular.

As time passed, many people—myself included—could not imagine this space going back to being car-free only on a part-time basis. This led to a big two-year campaign to make it permanent, which I'm proud to have been one small part of.

Fast-forward to November 8, 2022, when San Francisco voters passed a ballot measure by more than 60 percent to create what's now called JFK Promenade.

The advocates for JFK Promenade are *all* heroes of the park: local nonprofits and campaign volunteers, Mayor Breed, State Senator Scott Wiener, staff and leadership at the Recreation & Parks Department and the San Francisco Municipal Transportation Agency, including Phil Ginsburg and Jeffrey Tumlin, and supportive district supervisors. But it's David Miles Jr., who (like John McLaren) held strong to his vision through the years and kept speaking out for it. Known affectionately as the Mayor of Golden Gate Park, Miles continues to be one of the park's biggest promoters.

Walking around Blue Heron Lake and hiking Strawberry Hill in the middle is quite rewarding on a sunny day, with a view of the Golden Gate Bridge awaiting you at the top. *(Photo by Robert Ho)*

Huntington Falls. There are a couple of ways to climb to the very top of Strawberry Hill: one is straight up along the falls, another is a sloped path that goes around the back of the hill, and then there are other, smaller paths. From the top, you'll get views of downtown and the Golden Gate Bridge, possibly see some butterflies, and find the ruins of an observatory that crumbled in the 1906 earthquake. Blue Heron Lake has good bird-watching, and great blue herons nest on the islands from January through June (more on p. 138). The current boathouse was built in 1949; it can be rented for events and often hosts intimate jazz concerts on weekends.

GETTING THERE

The free Golden Gate Park Shuttle has a stop here. Free on-street parking can be found along Blue Heron Drive East. Blue Heron Lake is an easy walk from the Music Concourse.

Spreckels Lake and the San Francisco Model Yacht Club

The oldest model yacht club in the country is still going strong on a lake made specifically for miniature boats.

ADDRESS: JFK Drive and 36th Avenue

WEBSITE: sfmyc.org

HOURS: Spreckels Lake is open during park hours. Miniature sailboats and electric- and steam-powered boats are always allowed. There are some restrictions in terms of hours and days of the week that gas- and nitro-powered boats can be on the water. You don't have to be a member of the San Francisco Model Yacht Club to use your watercraft on Spreckels Lake.

AMENITIES: There is a public restroom open daily at the Model Yacht Clubhouse. On weekends, an Annie's Hot Dogs stand is usually set up at the lakeside.

The park is full of communities of people who have found each other through something they're passionate about. One of these is the sailors of miniature sailboats, speedboats, steamboats, and tugboats on Spreckels Lake. The lake is one of the few anywhere built specifically for model boats, and it is the place to be for hobbyists. It was completed in 1904, and a new clubhouse was built in 1937 as a federal Works Progress Administration project to provide jobs during the Great Depression.

The San Francisco Model Yacht Club continues a tradition that's been going on in the park since 1898: free-sailing three- to six-foot-long wooden boats. If you go inside the clubhouse, which is occasionally open to the public, you can check out some beautiful,

Spreckels Lake was created in 1904 specifically for miniature sailboats, and there's no shortage of wind in the park to fill their sails. Many types of powered boats now use the lake, too. *(Photo by Jim Watkins)*

handmade boats that date back to 1939. The freesail boats traverse the lake with no power source except the wind. Three types of freesail boats regularly race on the lake, and the best times to watch are Tuesdays, Wednesdays, Thursdays, and weekends, on the north side of the lake. The annual Model Boats on Parade event is in mid-September, and there's a Christmas lighted boat parade in mid-December. There are also regattas most weekends year-round. Go to sfmyc.org for a complete schedule.

GETTING THERE

The 5 and 5R Muni bus stop is less than a block away at Fulton Street and 36th Avenue. There is on-street parking along JFK Drive and at the nearby Polo Field parking lot.

Playgrounds

The park has six playgrounds. Of the six, the Koret Children's Quarter playground is the most popular destination for families citywide and beyond. The playgrounds are listed below, from east to west.

Panhandle Playground

ADDRESS: Oak Street and Ashbury Street in the Panhandle
AMENITIES: There are restrooms with changing tables, as well as picnic tables, which parties can reserve but the tables are often free. There's limited parking on Oak and Fell Streets and nearby residential streets.

This fully enclosed playground was renovated in 2019 and makes the most of this relatively small space. Whether or not to include sand in the new design was a major debate, but the pro-sand faction won, and there's now a contained sand area with buried sculptures. This playground is a hotspot for the baby-and-toddler crowd in the mornings, and many local elementary kids come by in late afternoons. It's easy to keep an eye on kids here even when it's crowded. Older elementary kids will find less to do here; it's better to head to Koret Children's Quarter playground with them.

Koret Children's Quarter and Carousel

ADDRESS: MLK Drive and Bowling Green Drive

AMENITIES: There are restrooms with changing tables at the top of the hill, and food and drinks at the California Kahve kiosk, which also sells carousel tickets (see p. 96; hours vary). There is very limited parking in the lot at the Lawn Bowling Club and more parking on nearby park roads, including Bowling Green Drive, MLK Drive, and Nancy Pelosi Drive. There is bike parking underneath the Sharon Art Studio and on the eastern end of the playground.

This premier playground dates back to 1888. When it first opened, it made history as the first public playground in America! In the early decades, kids enjoyed not only slides, swings, and a carousel but also cart rides pulled over the years by goats, donkeys, zebras, and even elephants. The concrete chutes built into the hill are from the 1970s; riding these on cardboard is recommended (there are usually some pieces at the bottom of the slide).

The Koret Children's Playground is a "destination playground," with multiple play areas (just one of which is shown here), plus the carousel.

The most recent renovation was in 2007, and it added features that ensure older kids will have fun here, too, like the climbing wave and giant rope-climbing structure. The renovation was when the name changed from the Sharon Quarters for Children to Koret Children's Quarter. The playground is big and busy on the weekends, making it harder to keep an eye on younger kids. But it's definitely the best playground in the park, popular with locals and beyond. There is also an accessible swing.

The historic **carousel** dates back to 1912, though it didn't arrive here in the park until 1941 (there were two previous carousels in its place; see more in "The Sharon Building and Children's Quarter" sidebar below). From Memorial Day to Labor Day, it's open daily from 10:30 a.m. to 4:30 p.m. on weekdays and 10 a.m. to 5 p.m. on weekends. After Labor Day, it's open Wednesday through Sunday with the same hours. Kids under five ride free. Get carousel tickets at the small building between the carousel and the Sharon Art Studio. This is concessionaire **California Kahve**, which has excellent coffee, pastries, sandwiches, and more.

The Sharon Building and Children's Quarter

Early on, William Hammond Hall identified the need for a dedicated part of the park for children. But it would take years until this would happen. Hall got his big chance in 1885 when the park commission was deciding how to use $50,000 that William Sharon had left to the park in his will. Hall, who was advising the park at this point, made a passionate case for an area with a playground (a brand-new idea at the time), a building for families (called the Sharon House for Children), and a carousel. Hall ultimately got his way.

Completed in 1888, the Sharon Building was "fully equipped with water fountains, ice cream fountains, soda places, dairy rooms, storerooms for playthings, and stables in the cellar for goats." The playground was the first public playground in America. It opened up with swings, slides, and seesaws in the early years, plus goat cart rides (which explains the goat stables). There was a big carousel under a tent powered by steam with stationary horses; a new carousel with horses that rocked replaced this a couple of years later when the domed structure you see today was built.

The Sharon Building was significantly damaged in the 1906 earthquake, with the area around it used as one of the

The Blue Playground

ADDRESS: 10th Avenue and Fulton Street

AMENITIES: The closest restrooms are a five- to ten-minute walk to behind the Bandshell on the Music Concourse. There is extremely limited on-street parking on Fulton Street.

Not-so-originally named for the color of most of its equipment, this oft-missed playground is somewhat hidden in its sunken location. Rarely too crowded, it's popular with neighboring families and is a friendly spot that has just enough monkey bars and slides to keep things interesting. If you're enjoying a day on JFK Promenade, this is worth adding as a stop. It's also connected to the Music Concourse via a long,

The Sharon Building and Children's Quarter opened in 1888 and was the first public playground in America. *(Photo by Jim Watkins)*

park's refugee camps. In the 1940s, farm animals were brought in; the barn and barnyard near the carousel are remnants of this time. Today, the Sharon Building is known as the Sharon Art Studio and offers a range of classes for youths and adults. Learn more at sharonartstudio.org. Take the time to walk the upper balcony to take in the architecture and views.

Mothers' Meadow Playground is a good choice on windy days—so, a lot of days!

beautifully carved tunnel created circa 1896 (see if you can find the bison heads in it!) that's fun for kids on scooters and bikes.

Mothers' Meadow Playground

ADDRESS: 569 MLK Drive (near Crossover Drive and 19th Avenue)
AMENITIES: You'll find restrooms with changing tables, plus picnic tables (which are reservable for parties). There's some on-street parking on MLK Drive. There is also bike parking.

This playground is from another era, with wooden and metal equipment surrounded by an ocean of sand. But it's beloved and a lot of fun, with excellent swings and climbing structures. The giant, sloping meadow surrounding it provides extra space to kick a ball or play tag far from the street. As a bonus, this playground may be the warmest one in the park in the mornings because nothing blocks the sun and it's somewhat protected from wind.

The Boat Playground at 45th Avenue

ADDRESS: 4414 Lincoln Way (Lincoln Way and 45th Avenue)

AMENITIES: You'll find restrooms with changing tables, plus picnic tables (which are reservable for parties). There is limited on-street parking on Lincoln Way; a free parking lot is half a mile away on Chain of Lakes Drive. There is also bike parking.

This is one of only two playgrounds west of Crossover Drive, and is practically all the way to the ocean. This quaint playground is mostly used by families who live nearby and appreciate its old-school style, which like Mothers' Meadow is from the wood-and-metal era. It includes plenty of sand that a blue metal boat is sunk into (the origins of the boat are a mystery). With excellent swings, a friendly vibe, and no other playgrounds within a mile (except the one listed below), this spot is usually hopping.

Playground at Beach Chalet Athletic Fields

ADDRESS: 1500 JFK Drive

AMENITIES: You'll find restrooms with changing tables, plus picnic tables (which are reservable). There is a free parking lot next to the field and on-street parking nearby on JFK Drive. There is bike parking.

This miniature playground almost didn't make the cut, but my kids love these play structures. And if you're in the area, why not add this in? It's just a quarter mile from the Boat Playground on foot.

An Adventure Tale Inspired by Golden Gate Park

If you love Golden Gate Park, you're in good company with Pulitzer Prize–winning (and local) author Dave Eggers. Eggers has said that Golden Gate Park is the best urban park in the world, and you'll find no arguments against that proclamation here. Eggers's all-ages book *The Eyes and the Impossible* is set in a *very* similar park, complete with bison, windmills, and true wildness. This animal adventure, and winner of the Newbery Medal, is an extra-fun read if you know the park well, as Eggers clearly does.

The Music Concourse Bandshell, built in 1900, hosts free concerts regularly, including by the longtime Golden Gate Park Band. *(Photo by Jim Watkins)*

Music and Events

Music has been part of the park since its creation. The first bandstand was built in the early 1880s for Sunday afternoon concerts. (That bandstand is no longer, well, standing). By 1900, the Spreckels Temple of Music (a.k.a. the **Bandshell**) in the **Music Concourse** offered a much bigger outdoor concert space, with seating at the time for 20,000. The Bandshell has been the backdrop for countless musical performances since, as well as historic civic gatherings, like a visit by President Harry Truman in 1948 where spectators watched dozens of warplanes fly overhead.

At this point, every type of music has echoed through the park. Opera legends like Luciano Pavarotti and Marilyn Horne have sung arias at Opera in the Park. The Grateful Dead, Jefferson Airplane, Jimi Hendrix, and Janis Joplin rocked out here, setting the 1960s music scene on fire. And major annual music festivals like Hardly Strictly Bluegrass and Outside Lands have brought a parade of musicians far too numerous and diverse to list.

The park's musical history is kept alive and well by the **Golden Gate Park Band**. They've played in the park since the time of that very first bandstand. You can enjoy their free concerts on Sundays at the Bandshell, usually from late April through early October (check the schedule at goldengateparkband.org). Each year, they host a two-day concert band festival in June. Besides the Golden Gate Park Band, there are free concerts of all genres on many afternoons and evenings at the Bandshell nearly **year-round**. The best way to find out what's playing is to go to illuminate.org or check San Francisco Recreation & Parks's social media or newsletter.

Tunnel Musicians, Buskers, Sing-Alongs, and More

Music is definitely one of the forms of magic you can stumble on in the park. One of the best places to look for small-scale live music is in **the tunnel in front of the Conservatory of Flowers**. The tunnel's excellent acoustics led to it being dubbed the "Conservatory of Music." There are often excellent jazz sessions on Friday afternoons and weekends.

The public **pianos on JFK Promenade** host impromptu performances (don't be shy). Stop by the piano at JFK Promenade where it meets Blue Heron Drive on Sunday afternoons for a community jam session. Especially on the weekends, you will often find acoustic musicians **along JFK Promenade**, including at the seasonal beer garden called the Whale's Tail. If you'd like to busk yourself, there is a program for permitted busking in various locations in the park.

Flower Piano in the Botanical Garden

It feels like humankind has reached its full potential when you're at Flower Piano. For about a week and a half in **September**, you can wander the Botanical Garden while every kind of music is played on pianos temporarily scattered throughout. Between scheduled concerts by top-notch pianists, the pianos are open to all, which brings a spontaneous aspect to the event that's really fun. This very popular event can be packed, so attend in the mornings and on weekdays if you can—and seek out the pianos in the farthest corners for the most intimate experiences. Most of Flower Piano's offerings are free for Botanical Garden members and San Francisco residents. Visit gggp.org/flowerpiano for information about the next Flower Piano.

Hardly Strictly Bluegrass

Back in 2001, local philanthropist Warren Hellman wanted to bring together some of his favorite bluegrass musicians to share with the city of San Francisco, so he funded a free, one-day celebration in the park called Strictly Bluegrass. Over the years, Hellman often referred to the event as "the world's most selfish gift" as it grew in scope: more days, more stages, and more types of roots music. The event became Hardly Strictly Bluegrass and is now a destination music festival attracting more than half a million people each year. In 2011, when Hellman died of leukemia, he left funding—and family members—committed to the festival, to continue "for as long as resources permit and the community desires." Hellman Hollow was named in his honor and, fittingly, is where the Banjo Stage is (Hellman was an accomplished banjo player).

The list of performers who have graced the stages at Hardly Strictly Bluegrass is impressive, including some of bluegrass music's all-time greats. Incredibly, Emmylou Harris has performed on the closing evening every year since 2001. Living in San Francisco, it's easy to take the festival for granted because it's free and right in our backyard. As it's grown and turned into more of a giant lawn party, it

Thanks to Warren Hellman, the park hosts a free music festival each year with bluegrass legends and musicians from other genres, too—hence the name Hardly Strictly Bluegrass.

can be frustrating when you hear more talking than the music itself. But when you're standing with tens of thousands of people singing your heart out as the sun sets behind the Towers of Gold stage and towering Monterey cypresses, you'd be crazy not to send a little prayer of thanks to Warren Hellman.

Hardly Strictly Bluegrass is usually the first weekend in **October**. Rules about what you can and can't bring to the festival change each year, so be sure to check the website at hardlystrictly bluegrass.com. You can also access videos, livestreams, and each year's list of performers.

Opera in the Park

The San Francisco Opera has hosted a free concert in the park since 1971, often with big stars and always a sing-along of "Libiamo ne' Lieti Calici" from *La Traviata* at the end. The concert is on a Sunday in early **September**. Held at Robin Williams Meadow, this is a chance to show off your most elegant picnic setup. Go to sfopera.com /operainthepark to get this year's date.

Outside Lands

Started in 2008, Outside Lands has become a destination music festival, with three days of acts on multiple stages and a lineup that always creates a buzz when it's announced in April.

Finding Fairy Doors

Fairy doors are scattered around the park in logs and trees. Some humans with an affinity for fairies make these for the magical creatures to take shelter behind. While the locations change over time, there are a couple that have been around for years. At the time of publication, fairy doors can be found:

- **In a Monterey cypress tree by Metson Lake.** If you're heading toward the lake from the east, look for a tall cypress tree on the left side of Middle Drive West. The fairy door is in the base of the trunk.
- **In the base of a London plane tree in the Music Concourse.** If you're facing the Music Concourse, look in a tree that's toward the front to the right.

Over time, it's moved away from including a few rock-and-roll icons that got the older generations to buy the pricey tickets and now mostly focuses on the hottest artists of the moment. If you go to its Wikipedia page, the list of musicians and bands featured since it started is pretty incredible.

Always in **August** (a.k.a. Fogust), the weather doesn't really match the mood of this youthful party of over 200,000 people. The event's name is a nod to what the western half of San Francisco was called in the 1800s before the park was created. I'm not sure how John McLaren would feel about using the park this way, but Outside Lands is a big fundraiser for San Francisco Recreation & Parks, as well as a local tourism booster. It's not so different from when the 1894 California Midwinter International Exposition came to the park. Learn more at outsidelands.org.

Annual Events in the Park

Beyond the music, there are other major events to know about—including some free ones you won't want to miss.

The biggest walking and running events that come through the park are the Hot Chocolate Run (**January**), the San Francisco Half Marathon (**February**), Bay to Breakers (**May**), the San Francisco Marathon (**July**), and the AIDS Walk (**July**).

At the end of **April**, Bay Area Dance Week brings a free, all-day event called **Dancing in the Park** to the Bandshell, showcasing a variety of companies, soloists, and styles. Also in late April, a holiday from the Netherlands—**King's Day**—celebrates Dutch culture and traditions at the Murphy Windmill, which gets to spin its sails that day.

Started in 1967 in the Haight-Ashbury neighborhood, the annual **Festival of Chariots** has been held in the park on one **summer** Sunday ever since. This event is part of a spiritual festival for a branch of Hinduism known to many as the Hare Krishna movement. Learn more at iskconberkeley.us. A parade of chariots is pulled down JFK Promenade before arriving in Robin Williams Meadow for a free vegetarian feast and other activities, all open to the public.

In **September**, a lineup of over fifty comedians performs for free at **Comedy Day in the Park**. This is held in Robin Williams Meadow, which was named in 2018 to memorialize the comedian who got his start in San Francisco and performed at the park's first Comedy Day in 1981. Comedians donate their time to this one-of-a-kind event. "The comics of San Francisco give you this free show because we love it here," said comedian Paula Poundstone in 2020. Aw, gotta love that!

Usually on the **first Thursday in December**, the park hosts the city's official **holiday tree lighting** at McLaren Lodge and along JFK Promenade. San Francsico Recreation & Parks goes all out with free carnival rides, live music, crafting activities, and more. This is a must for families with young kids. The current mayor is usually the one to flip the switch on the lights adorning the giant Monterey cypress known as "Uncle John's Tree." "Uncle John" is John McLaren, who oversaw the park for fifty-three years (more on p. 18); the tree-lighting tradition started in 1929 on his eighty-fourth birthday. Today, the event also includes a Hanukkah menorah and a Kwanzaa kinara.

Lastly, the Tony Award–winning **San Francisco Mime Troupe** does free performances in the park yearly. Check their website at sfmt.org to catch their bold and creative political satire.

Tips for Finding Even More Events

Beyond the biggies, there are countless additional events that are hard even for locals to track. Stopping by McLaren Lodge is a good way to find out what's going on that day, though the hours of the lodge are unpredictable. Signing up for San Francisco Recreation & Parks's weekly newsletter at sfrecpark.org (scroll to the bottom of the webpage) is helpful. The department's social media also often shares events at @sfrecpark on Instagram and @recparksf on X. I post many events at @secretgoldengatepark on Instagram, too.

But many activities, like ongoing **free Zumba classes** in the park, are often stumbled upon by chance. Or you can first identify the activity or attraction you're interested in and then go from there (for example, if you go to the Golden Gate Angling & Casting Club's website, you'll find when free classes are offered).

Throughout the year, the **San Francisco County Fair Building** hosts many public events (some with entry fees), from chocolate expositions to antique paper fairs to orchid shows, but there is unfortunately not a calendar online to see what's coming up. Doing a search in Eventbrite for "Golden Gate Park" within San Francisco will bring up some of the other happenings, too, like yoga classes and cultural celebrations open to the public. The website sf.funcheap.com is another good source.

As the city's largest public space, the park hosts countless events big and small. See what's on tap the next time you head there to find yet another way to enjoy the park.

Public Art

There is more art than ever outside the doors of the de Young Museum. Here's some of what you can find elsewhere in the park.

Sculptures and Art Installations

The park has several noteworthy outdoor art pieces, including the following:

- ***La Rose des Vents* gilded sculpture in front of the Conservatory of Flowers.** Installed in 2015, this work by French artist Jean-Michel Othoniel is inspired by a compass rose, which indicates the cardinal directions on a map and helps sailors gauge wind direction—and it indeed moves with the wind. Othoniel has said that he fell in love with the park on his first visit in 1999. Très bien!
- **Sculptures and art installations on and along JFK Promenade.** Starting in 2022, thanks to local nonprofit Illuminate in partnership with San Francisco Recreation & Parks, works have been installed on a temporary and more long-term basis. The "Love Blocks" sculptures near the Conservatory of Flowers and the submerged wooden whale sculpture on JFK Promenade next to the 14th Avenue East Meadow are here to stay, and hopefully the sea serpent Naga installed below Rainbow Falls in 2025 will, too. Learn more about the art on and near JFK Promenade at goldenmileproject.org.
- **Sculpture gardens on either end of the de Young Museum.** These include some classics, like the pair of sphinxes that have greeted parkgoers for more than a century, plus some don't-miss modern works. Learn more on p. 68.

Statues and Monuments

One way history is reflected in the park is by the many statues and monuments recognizing notable people and events, like memorials to those who died in World Wars I and II. A handful of statues were part of the 1894 California Midwinter International Exposition and never left: the Doré vase, the apple cider press statue, the sphinxes, and Leonidas (incorrectly called the "Roman gladiator" before finally being identified as the famous king of Sparta). Some are pretty random, like the Ludwig van Beethoven bust and the baseball player. Some *seem* random, like the

The *La Rose des Vents* gold sculpture in front of the Conservatory of Flowers is one of many pieces of public art to seek out.

Goethe-Schiller or the Verdi monuments, but were actually the efforts of immigrants in San Francisco paying tribute to their homelands.

Wealthy people loved donating statues to the park, especially during John McLaren's time—and there was a general sentiment that urban parks needed them. But McLaren wasn't a fan, believing that statues took away from the feeling of being in nature. He had gardeners plant trees and bushes to hide many of them, which is why even today you can still miss giant ones (like the aforementioned monument to Giuseppe Verdi at the western end of the Music Concourse).

While the statues and monuments mostly blend into the background of the park's greenery, you may want to seek out the following few for a closer look and contemplation:

The prominent James Garfield monument on the hill near the Conservatory of Flowers. Garfield was the twentieth president of the United States and was

The Francis Scott Key Memorial no longer holds the statue of Key himself.

assassinated in 1881. The statue of the woman on this monument, who is meant to represent the United States, is draped in a shroud and holds a sword with a broken blade. Within the cornerstone of the monument is a time capsule. This monument has been here since 1885, making it the oldest in the park.

The missing statue of Francis Scott Key, within the larger monument in the Music Concourse topped by the Goddess of Liberty. The Key statue was one of those taken down by protesters on Juneteenth in 2020. Key, who wrote the poem "The Star-Spangled Banner," which became the national anthem, was an enslaver who opposed ending slavery. The lyrics are inscribed on the base of the monument. Look for the bison heads near the top.

The statue of John McLaren in John McLaren Memorial Rhododendron Dell. This was presented to McLaren during his lifetime, but unsurprisingly, he didn't put it up in the park. After his death, it was installed in the dell planted in his honor. Follow **In the Steps of John McLaren** (see p. 160) to stand eye to eye with a likeness of the "Boss Gardener," knowing he wouldn't approve of the tribute.

More Art to Seek Out

The Helen Crocker Russell Library of Horticulture at the Botanical Garden, currently open to the public Friday through Sunday, has seasonal nature-themed art exhibits. Local artists with the Artists Guild of San Francisco and Red Umbrellas show their original work on weekends in the Music Concourse and at Alvord Lake (near Haight Street). And Beach Chalet, which is open to the public, features murals painted by Lucien Labaudt in 1935 and 1936 depicting scenes from the park and city at the time.

Athletics and Outdoor Activities

From the beginning, Golden Gate Park offered space not just for enjoying nature but also for being active. Some activities go back almost to the beginning of the park's history. Many have loyal communities of participants and, in true San Francisco style, are welcoming to newcomers.

Archery

LOCATION: Golden Gate Park Archery Range, 902 47th Avenue, south of Fulton Street

Way out in the far northwest corner of the park, the archery range is off the radar for most. But it gets more use than you'd think, including by practitioners of the ancient Japanese martial art of kyūdō archery. This wasn't the first location in the park for archery, but this field was established in 1938. Archery in the park goes back to 1881, and it was one of the rare sports at the time that allowed equal participation for women. By 1904, women were competing in archery at the Olympics!

WHAT TO KNOW: The range is free and open to the public, but you need to bring your own bow, arrows, and targets. Aim for a weekday, if you can, for fewer archers using the nine hay bales. San Francisco Recreation & Parks occasionally offers classes for youths here. City College of San Francisco also offers an adult archery class here. The Golden Gate Junior Olympic Archery Development is an all-volunteer club that teaches kids and adults; it holds practice here every Saturday morning and hosts occasional tournaments. Learn more at goldengatejoad.com.

Baseball

LOCATION: Big Rec Ball Field, 100 MLK Drive

America's pastime was already popular by the time the park was established. Conveniently, the California Midwinter International Exposition of 1894 flattened out a large area that became known as "Big Rec." Historical photos show Big Rec being used for baseball in 1905—and then, a year later, it was used for an encampment for people who had lost their homes in the 1906 earthquake. In 1960, baseball legend and local hero Joe DiMaggio coached kids and showed off his skills at the Big Rec.

WHAT TO KNOW: A variety of youth and adult leagues use the baseball fields, including a historically minded league called Bay Area Vintage Base Ball that

Baseball has been played in the park since 1905, and today you can watch vintage games with old-time rules and uniforms. *(Photo by Jim Watkins)*

plays by rules—and with equipment—from 1886. Look up their schedule at bavbb.com; the season runs March through September. Fields can be reserved through sfrecpark.org.

Basketball

LOCATION: Nate Thurmond Panhandle Basketball Courts in the Panhandle (at Fell and Clayton Streets)

Basketball was slow to catch on in San Francisco. Its presence in the park likely didn't get going until the Kezar Pavilion opened in 1927 and was used by local basketball teams. The outdoor court in the Panhandle was added sometime after cars were removed in 1955. It was refurbished in 2016 and named for Golden State Warriors legend Nate Thurmond.

WHAT TO KNOW: The courts in the Panhandle are for pick-up games. These are not reservable.

Bicycling

The modern bicycle was invented around 1885 and grew in popularity over the next ten years as mass production made bikes more affordable. San Franciscans, always early adopters, were buying the new models as soon as they came out and riding them to Golden Gate Park. Conflicts between early bicyclists and horses were resolved by banning bikes on nearly all park roads. But by 1894, bicycling had increased so much in popularity that the park not only allowed bikes on most roads but also built designated bike paths. (Some of these paths

Kezar Stadium and Kezar Pavilion

The original Kezar Stadium opened in 1925, and was enlarged a few years later to seat 59,000 people. *(Photo courtesy of Greg Gaar)*

The San Francisco 49ers pro football team played home games at Kezar Stadium from 1947 to 1970. The stadium was later demolished and rebuilt between 1989 and 1991 to seat 10,000 people versus almost 60,000 previously. You can see the original stadium in a scene from the classic Clint Eastwood film *Dirty Harry*. Today, the stadium is used for high school sports events (including the annual football championship game on Thanksgiving) and graduations, and it's a popular spot for runners due to its professional-grade track and lighting in the evenings. It's also the home of a new professional soccer team, Golden City Football Club.

Nearby is Kezar Pavilion, an indoor gymnasium for spectator sports mostly used for basketball games these days, but it has a storied history in roller derby. In 2014, Golden State Warriors basketball superstar **Stephen Curry** scored forty-three points in a San Francisco Bay Area Pro-Am Summer Basketball League game here. But Kezar Pavilion is also where the University of San Francisco Dons played during the days of **Bill Russell** in 1955 and 1956. Russell would go on to become one of basketball's all-time greats as a center with the Boston Celtics. He was the first African American coach in NBA history and a fierce advocate for racial justice.

are still used today, including the multiuse trail by Hellman Hollow and a few dirt roads in the western part of the park.)

Today, bicycling is part of the fabric of the park, including mountain biking, track cycling, and road and recreational biking. Many San Francisco kids learn to ride a bike on JFK Promenade. You can rent bikes in and around the park, including e-bikes and pedal-powered surreys. There is a seasonal program to provide adaptive bicycles for people with mobility limitations, too.

WHAT TO KNOW: In the 1960s and 1970s, **mountain biking** got its start as a sport just over the Golden Gate Bridge in Marin County. The park currently has 2.3 miles of dirt trails designated and marked as multiuse where mountain biking is allowed. Mountain bikers of all levels can be found on these relatively flat trails. Going off-trail is a no-go because the sandy soil is easily impacted by bikes. Refer to the map below for trail locations, or learn more at sfrecpark.org.

Track cycling is exactly what it sounds like, and Golden Gate Park happens to have a large outdoor oval track for this sport: the **Polo Field** (a.k.a. Golden Gate

Park Stadium). From its start in 1906, the Polo Field had a bicycle track, and it is considered the oldest cycling track in the United States. Track racing was popular here through the 1950s, with competitors riding bikes with one gear and no brakes! The cycle track at the Polo Field is usually available, but not when there are events in the Polo Field, so check sfrecpark.org/calendar to view the daily cycle track hours. It's 0.7 mile around. You don't need to be trying to break records to use the track; it's open to all speeds of cyclists.

The park has over 15 miles of roadways within its borders. Happily, more than 4 miles are car-free—ideal for **road and recreational riding**. You can ride almost entirely across the park without dealing with vehicle traffic, all the way to the Pacific Ocean. **Road cyclists**, who tend to be spandex-wearing types on bikes built for speed, often meet in and ride through the park on their way to longer rides around the city or over the Golden Gate Bridge into the Marin Headlands. Many local bike shops have road cycling clubs and are a good place to start for finding a group ride that's your speed. The rest of us are the many **recreational and commuter bicyclists** riding in the park for fun and transportation. Beginners feel comfortable learning and riding here, particularly on the car-free roads, and riding a bike is the most efficient way to get around the park.

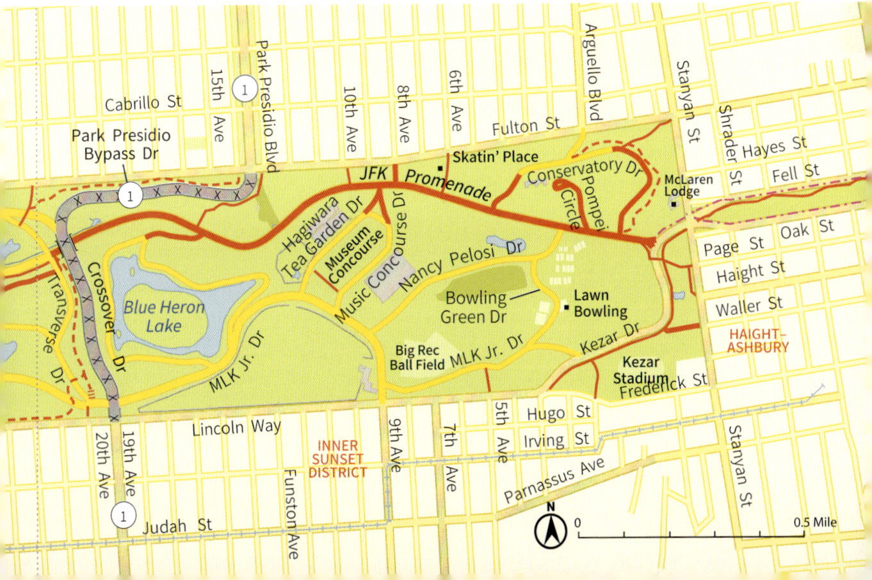

Bocce

LOCATION: Bocce courts, 601 Stanyan Street near Alvord Lake

Bocce, an ancient game that made its way to the United States in the early 1900s, is the simplest of the ball-rolling options in the park (check out Lawn Bowling and Pétanque below).

Two bocce courts were finally added to the park in 2020. With overhead lighting at night, you can enjoy a smooth court anytime at this charming, low-key spot.

WHAT TO KNOW: Recreational bocce leagues occasionally use the courts, but otherwise they are first-come, first-served and not too busy. Bring your own bocce balls. During the day, Flywheel Coffee operates out of the small building next to the bocce courts. There's also an all-gender public restroom next to the courts.

Disc Golf

LOCATION: 99 Marx Meadow Drive

Golden Gate Park is full of passionate communities. The story behind disc golf in the park is a perfect example. Volunteers came together to fund and build the eighteen-hole disc golf course (the first in the city) in 2007, and they continue to maintain it as the San Francisco Disc Golf Club.

Invented in the 1970s, disc golf is similar to traditional golf. You throw your first disc from a tee area, then keep throwing from where it lands until you get it into the basket (with a point or stroke for each toss). Like golf pars for each hole, each disc golf basket has a par for the number of tosses it should take you to score. Some holes require you to toss on a certain side of a tree! Players use discs of different sizes and weights depending on the throw, like how golfers use different clubs. Don't be intimidated if you're a beginner; you're welcome here. However, if you're more serious, there are also clinics and tournaments. Every Sunday morning, there's a singles league. Learn more and sign up at sfdiscgolf.org.

WHAT TO KNOW: This course is open to the public, has no tee times, and is free to use. However, you need to bring your own discs (you can use a traditional frisbee, but it's not ideal). Sports Basement sells three-disc sets for around $30 to $40; you would ideally have a putter, a midrange, and a driver disc. The course tends to be busier on weekends, especially Sunday mornings. Weekdays and Saturday mornings are quieter. You can read the full rules and etiquette, plus get a printable scorecard, at sfdiscgolf.org. There is an active San Francisco Disc Golf Club Facebook group, as well as related groups for buying and selling discs and for women's club members. Showing up with some discs on a weekend is a great way to jump into this sport and community.

Fly Casting at the Anglers Lodge and Casting Pools

LOCATION: Anglers Lodge and casting pools, 1232 JFK Drive

Tucked in the west side of the park near the Polo Field, you may be surprised to find a series of pools built especially for the sport of fly casting. Fly casting became popular in the late 1800s in the United States and stayed that way for many decades, in part because movie stars and American presidents liked fly fishing. Fly casting (which is fly fishing minus the actual fish) started in Golden Gate Park at Blue Heron Lake in the late 1800s. The sport had traveled west with the Gold Rush, especially through people from Scotland and England. In 1938, casting pools were built in the park. The following year, the rustic wooden Anglers Lodge was completed as a federal Works Progress Administration project. The lodge is generally open for viewing during events; club members may let you take a look inside on other days.

Built in 1938, the fly casting pools have produced world champions (but never any fish). *(Photo by Jim Watkins)*

Over the decades, many national and international competitions testing distance and accuracy have been held at the casting pools. Many champions have come from these pools, too. A local girl named Maxine McCormick started fly casting here at age nine. McCormick became a wunderkind of the sport, winning her first international gold medal in 2016 when she was just twelve, beating both men and women. She has since won more golds. Club members point out, however, that McCormick is one of many champions in the club's long history. Each April, the annual world championship in Spey casting is held here. A handful of rock stars, local and otherwise, have quietly enjoyed casting at this hidden spot over the years. Because the casting pools are a rarity, they're a destination for those in the know.
WHAT TO KNOW: The Golden Gate Angling & Casting Club occupies the Anglers Lodge and oversees events at the casting pools, including lessons and fly-tying classes. However, the pools are public, so unless an event is happening, you can show up with gear and cast away. Once a month—usually the second Saturday—the club offers a free fly-casting class for the public. Register early to help the club plan for enough instructors, and try to arrive before 9 a.m. if you plan to use the free loaner equipment (bring some kind of eye protection, even just sunglasses). Instructors are friendly and welcoming to newbies, so don't be surprised if you get asked to join the club. Members get to hang out in the Anglers Lodge, among other perks. Check out the event calendar at ggacc.org. There are public restrooms.

Golf

LOCATION: Golden Gate Park Golf Course, 970 47th Avenue

In the far northwestern corner of the park is an affordable, nine-hole, par-three public golf course with a small driving range and a peek at the Pacific Ocean. Most parkgoers will never stumble upon it (and non-golfers are not allowed on the course green itself). Holes range from under one hundred yards to two hundred yards, and the course has fun slopes, thanks to the sand dunes it's built on and a 2023 update by architect Jay Blasi. It can be played in less than an hour, and golfers of all levels find the course fun and challenging. If you get a hole-in-one, it will be logged and celebrated!

WHAT TO KNOW: The course is open daily. Online tee times are required and book up quickly, but you can pay a modest extra fee to book more than a week in advance—and this is very highly recommended. Weekday mornings are about the only time you are likely to walk on to the course. To take advantage of the San

With views of the Pacific Ocean, reasonable prices, and a redesigned course, this is a gem for all levels of golfers.

Francisco–resident greens fee, you need a San Francisco Resident Golf Card. You can apply online, but it takes a few weeks. You can also go in person to TCP Harding Park on certain days. Either way, only pursue this if you plan to golf a lot, or else it doesn't make sense financially. Learn more at sfrecpark.org.

Each golfer must have their own set of clubs, golf bag, and putter (no sharing); these can be rented at the clubhouse, which is one of the hidden gems of the park. Anyone can enjoy it, including the lovely patio seating overlooking the course. Not only can you buy balls and rent a pull cart, you can also buy food and drinks, including beer, the famous Hot Dog Bills Burgerdog, and coffee and pastries. The 2023 renovation added nice all-gender restrooms, too. There's also free Wi-Fi. Learn more at ggpgolf.org or call (415) 751-8987 or email info@ggpgolf.org. Instruction for youths aged six to seventeen is available through firstteesanfrancisco.org.

Handball and Racquetball

LOCATION: Handball courts, right off of Nancy Pelosi Drive behind the Big Rec Ball Field (at 100 MLK Drive)

It was Irish immigrants who brought handball to San Francisco in the late 1800s. As handball caught on as a game for everyone, the park installed its first courts in the late 1920s. The courts you'll find today were built in 1958 and are for both handball and what was a new sport at the time: racquetball. This bare-bones building is usually pretty quiet, reflecting the decline in overall popularity of these two sports. But the back of the building is a great place to hit tennis balls against a wall.

WHAT TO KNOW: Two open-air and two enclosed handball/racquetball courts are free and available on a first-come, first-served basis.

Horseback Riding

LOCATION: Bercut Equitation Field at the corner of MLK Drive and Chain of Lakes Drive

Horses helped create Golden Gate Park. They pulled plows to grade the sand dunes, and their manure from downtown city streets was crucial in fertilizing the sandy soil to support trees. Later on, horses pulled carriages and carts full of visitors to the park, and they raced in Speedway Meadow (now called Hellman Hollow) and at the Polo Field. While horses are a relatively rare sight in the park today, some people bring their horses in from outside the city. Mounted police are also occasionally spotted; their horses are housed at the police stables next to the Polo Field. Horseback riding lessons and trail rides have been available to the public in recent years at the Bercut Equitation Field; this will hopefully be the case again soon. The park stables, built in 1939, once offered riding lessons to the public. But they've been closed since 2001, requiring costly major renovations to be usable again.

WHAT TO KNOW: There is currently no vendor in the park for horseback riding.

Horseshoes

LOCATION: Horseshoe courts off of Conservatory Drive East, near the Hayes Street and Stanyan Street entrance to the park

Tucked away up some trails in the northeast corner of the park is a nearly forgotten area for throwing horseshoes. Built in 1927, when this lawn game was a popular pastime, it's mostly a thing of the past now, with very occasional use.

WHAT TO KNOW: The rules are simple for this kid-friendly and social game. These days, there are rubber, light-up, and many other options for horseshoes available online. Note that the metal posts you throw the horseshoes at are permanently installed. Only a few of the courts are maintained, with dirt around the posts instead of overgrown grass. You'll likely have this area to yourself if you go. There's an old sculpture of someone tossing a horseshoe carved into the wall behind the courts, and you can see how this area was mined for chert rock, which was used to pave the park in its early days.

Lawn Bowling

LOCATION: 320 Bowling Green Drive

How is it that San Francisco is home to the oldest public lawn bowling greens and club in America? It turns out that long-time park superintendent John McLaren loved the game, which shared his Scottish roots. He was instrumental to the installation of the park's first bowling green in 1902, and he played plenty of games himself over the years. The nation's first women's lawn bowling club started here in 1912 (eventually these clubs merged).

WHAT TO KNOW: While you can't walk onto the bowling green unless you're a member, don't let that make you think the San Francisco Lawn Bowling Club is an exclusive scene. And you don't need to wear white: that's just for tournaments, and even that's optional these days. The club offers free lessons on a request basis for ages twelve and up, and as soon as you complete three lessons, you can join the club (dues are required). Membership perks include regular games, monthly social events, and access to the vintage 1916 clubhouse and meticulously manicured bowling greens.

Lawn bowling uses asymmetrical, three-pound "bowls" that can be borrowed from the club, though most people have their own. The size and shape of the bowls make the game challenging. "Bocce is for kids, lawn bowling is for grownups," one bowler told me. Members range in age from twelve to over ninety! Wondering about those big nets laying across the lawn? Those are "long mats" to protect the delicate surface from indentations when bowls are tossed, especially during the wet season. Just want to watch bowlers in action? There are regular "draw" games for members on Tuesdays, Thursdays, and Saturdays at 10 a.m. and 12:15 p.m., plus occasional tournaments. Learn more at sflbc.org.

Lindy Dancing

Lindy in the Park has been going strong since 1996. You can find free swing dancing on the bridge on JFK Promenade near the de Young Museum every Sunday from 11 a.m. to 2 p.m. A free half-hour lesson is at noon. This fun, friendly community is open to all ages and levels. Volunteer DJs spin a mix of jazz, blues, and swing music. Be prepared to switch partners after each song; dancers quickly share if they are a "leader" or "follower," regardless of gender identity, to pair up with someone new. Learn more at lindyinthepark.com.

Parcourse

LOCATION: Near the upper dirt loop in the Polo Field. The first station—the Achilles Stretch with a "welcome" sign—is near the eastern side of the parking lot at the southwest corner of the Polo Field.

It was 1973 when a local named Peter Stocker brought a European idea to San Francisco: outdoor fitness stations in parks. He installed the first "parcourse" at

Every Sunday afternoon, you can take a free swing dance lesson and join the fun of Lindy in the Park. *(Photo by Jim Watkins)*

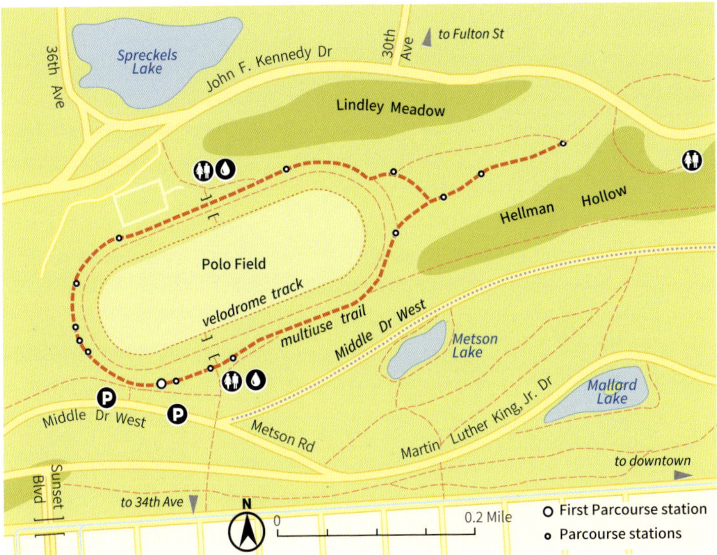

Mountain Lake Park, about a mile from Golden Gate Park. Parcourse brought the gym to the people. But "par" isn't for "park"—it's for the number of repetitions recommended to get a full workout. Parcourse took off in the fitness-loving 1980s, and soon courses were everywhere in America, including a fifteen-station parcourse near the Polo Field. See the map above for the locations.

WHAT TO KNOW: This "fitness trail" is 1.3 miles long and well maintained. There is a specific order in which to complete the stations to get you warmed up before it becomes more challenging. The route goes counterclockwise around the Polo Field, with an additional short spur off this loop. Doing the full parcourse is a full-body workout. It takes thirty to forty-five minutes and the equipment is never busy—though maybe it will be now that this book has put it on the map!

Pétanque

LOCATION: The pétanque playing field is just south of 6251 Fulton Street, across the parking lot from the Golden Gate Park Dog Training Area.

The pétanque playing field is easy to miss, and you've probably never heard of pétanque, despite its widespread popularity in France. But the field in the park dates back to 1959, and was the first court on the West Coast.

While this outdoor French lawn game shares the basic "throw bigger balls toward a smaller one" concept of bocce and lawn bowling, it has other strategies to it, including going after opponents.

"Bocce is to checkers as pétanque is to chess," said one of the members of La Boule d'Or Pétanque Club in Golden Gate Park (though when I told this to a lawn bowler, they said the pétanque players stole this line from them). Like all the communities in the park, this is a friendly one.

WHAT TO KNOW: Free lessons are offered from La Boule d'Or Pétanque Club, and kids are welcome. Go to sfpetanque.org to request a lesson; equipment is provided. If you already play pétanque and want to join the fun, there are meetups to play casual games on Wednesdays at 10:30 a.m., Fridays at 2 p.m., and Sundays at 10:30 a.m.

Tennis, Pickleball, and Table Tennis (Ping-Pong)

LOCATION: Lisa and Douglas Goldman Tennis Center, 10 Bowling Green Drive at Nancy Pelosi Drive

Tennis was invented in 1873, just a few years after Golden Gate Park was established. Whoever laid out the first couple of dirt tennis courts in the park in 1894 probably couldn't have imagined how things would go for the new sport (perhaps like the three men who came up with pickleball in 1965). But tennis took off quickly, and by the early 1920s, the park had many courts—plus the first clubhouse, at the site of what's now the Lisa and Douglas Goldman Tennis Center.

The Lisa and Douglas Goldman Tennis Center has sixteen tennis courts and five pickleball courts open to the public for a fee. *(Photo by Jim Watkins)*

The park would prove important for the evolution of tennis in terms of how it's played and *who* plays. It has nurtured incredible talent from all backgrounds on the public courts. It started what's now known as the US Gay Open. Hall-of-famers Billie Jean King, Rosie Casals, Brad Gilbert, Dick Gould, and Peanut Louie Harper all played here. The Lisa and Douglas Goldman Tennis Center hosts the San Francisco City Championships, also known as the SF Open—one of the oldest tennis competitions in the nation. And the public is always invited to watch!

In 2021, the $27 million Goldman Tennis Center was completed, including a beautiful clubhouse with sixteen tennis courts and five designated pickleball courts. The new center kept the previous clubhouse's long tradition of table tennis, too.

WHAT TO KNOW: Generally, you need a reservation for these popular courts. You may get lucky with a walk-on between 7 a.m. and 9 a.m., but your odds drop quickly after that. After 4 p.m. and especially on weekdays, there's almost no chance for a walk-on court. If you're a resident, you can reserve courts eight days in advance; for nonresidents, it's seven days. You can make reservations online at goldmantennis center.com, by phone at (415) 581-2540, or in person. No matter what, you'll need an account to use a court or make a reservation. You're charged when you check in to play. If you're a San Francisco resident, there's a discount, so bring proof of residency the first time you play.

Bring your own equipment, or buy what you need from the pro shop (no rentals) for tennis and pickleball. There are a wide range of lessons, workshops, and camps for all ages and skill levels. There is no wall to use for solo play; however, just a few blocks away behind the handball courts is one that's rarely used. As for table tennis, the one table here requires reservations (and a fee). But it's often empty, so you can walk in and then sign up to play right away. There are lessons on Saturdays for all ages. Note that there are free outdoor table-tennis tables with public equipment available on JFK Promenade at 8th Avenue.

The courts open at 7 a.m. and are lit and open until 10 p.m. every day. The Goldman Tennis Center has very nice restrooms (including an all-gender restroom), an outdoor patio, and free Wi-Fi. There is an affordable coffee and hot chocolate machine inside, plus vending machines, tables, and couches. It also has what's probably the most secure bike parking in the park: You can bring your bike through the building to racks next to the courts. There's also plentiful bike parking outside the center.

Thanks to David Miles Jr. (center with top hat), there's a designated roller rink in the park and a true San Francisco experience waiting for you. *(Photo by Jim Watkins)*

Roller-Skating

LOCATION: Skatin' Place, 6th Avenue between JFK Drive and Fulton Street

People have been roller-skating in the park since its early days. Believe it or not, the park's first roller rink (now long gone) was installed in 1891! But it was the 1970s when the craze fully descended on San Francisco, with 20,000 people roller-skating in the park on a given weekend. The popularity of roller-skating created a backlash, with some people wanting to ban it in the park. Thanks to the efforts of David Miles Jr., that didn't happen. Miles organized volunteer safety patrols to monitor and help skaters, while also fighting against a ban (read more about David Miles Jr., a hero of the park, on p. 90). The patrols also pushed for the eventual creation of the permanent rink built in 1984: Skatin' Place.

Today, Skatin' Place is a welcoming scene that draws beginners of all ages, plus some of the best roller and inline skaters around. Wednesday evenings and Sunday afternoons are when the skate community comes out in full force. Friday nights—or any warm evening—are often a full skate-party scene, complete with a DJ. Near Halloween, there's a Friday night costumed skate that's a true San Francisco experience. Skatin' Place has been described as a "joy vortex," and even if you just stop to watch, you'll definitely feel that!

WHAT TO KNOW: Skatin' Place is free and open to the public during park hours. If you're a beginner or have young kids, it's best to go during non-peak times. Weekdays anytime (except Friday evenings) or weekends before 10 a.m. are generally quiet.

Be sure to skate in the same direction as the other skaters, give them plenty of space, and avoid cutting across the rink. Slower skaters should stay closer to the center. If you want lessons, there are longtime teachers who give lessons at Skatin' Place, including ones for kids—just ask around on a weekend. Group lessons are also offered at an indoor private rink called the Church of 8 Wheels, which can provide teacher referrals. Each summer, usually in July, San Francisco celebrates Skate Week, organized by the Church of 8 Wheels. One event is a not-to-be-missed Sunday showcase of singles, couples, and groups at Skatin' Place. Learn more at churchof8wheels.com.

Running

Many world-class runners have pounded the park's pavement and paths over the years, in great part because Bay to Breakers, the San Francisco Half Marathon, and the San Francisco Marathon go through the park. The USA Track & Field National Club Cross Country Championships have also been held here several times. Olympians Cole Hocker, Marisa Howard, Shannon Rowbury (a San Franciscan), Jennifer Rhines, Bridget Franek, Magdalena Lewy-Boulet, and David Torrence have all raced in the park.

JFK Promenade is of course popular with runners, with plenty of room for large groups. It is 1.5 miles one-way along the length of JFK Promenade, but you can continue along the network of car-free and car-light spaces in the park, which is 3 miles one-way (see the map on p. 112). The 0.7-mile Panhandle sees plenty of runners; note that the path on the south side doesn't allow bicycles, so it can be more enjoyable for jogging. The outermost loop around Blue Heron Lake is exactly 1 mile. Middle Lake has a 0.4-mile loop. Trail running is also excellent in the park, given the huge network of dirt paths, many of which skirt the perimeter of the park.

TRACK RUNNING

Kezar Stadium, which is lit at night, has a professional-grade, 400-meter track but also a wide, paved upper track that's about 0.4 mile per lap. There are public restrooms here and plenty of stairs for workouts. The Polo Field has a dirt track on the upper edge of the oval that is 0.8 mile per loop, but there's no lighting for evening runs. There are public restrooms on either side of the Polo Field. While you're there, you can use the parcourse stations nearby for workouts.

SUPPORTED RUNS AND THE RUNNING COMMUNITY

San Francisco has no shortage of running clubs and organized runs to motivate you. Go to sfruns.com for a directory of clubs and upcoming events. From the Hot Chocolate Run to over forty local charity walks and runs to a Turkey Trot on Thanksgiving morning, there's rarely a weekend without something to sign up for in the park. During San Francisco's Pride weekend in June each year, there are 5K and 10K walks and runs to celebrate and support the LGBTQIA+ community; these are open to all. Learn more at sffr.org.

Five Ways to Travel Back in Time in the Park

1 **Experience old-fashioned sports and pastimes.** Look up the schedule for the Bay Area Vintage Base Ball league and catch a game. Lawn bowling, archery, and fly casting have all been enjoyed in the park since the Victorian era.

2 **Visit the Conservatory of Flowers.** Built in 1879, this is the oldest structure in the park, and you can feel this (in a good way). The giant water lily exhibit was a big deal in the Conservatory's early years; visitors can enjoy the same exhibit today.

3 **Rent a boat in Blue Heron Lake.** Visitors have been paddling boats around this lake since 1893.

4 **Go hear the Golden Gate Park Band.** This band has played in the park since 1882! Its first concerts were in a little bandstand that people would pull their horse carriages up to. The band has played at the Bandshell on the Music Concourse since 1886.

Skateboarding

LOCATION: Zion Skate Park at Stanyan Street and Waller Street, near the Haight Street entrance to the park

Skateboarding was born in California, created by surfers in San Diego in the 1950s who wanted something to do when there weren't good waves to ride. But in the 1980s and 1990s, it was San Francisco where street skating came to life. A new world of tricks and skater culture emerged in our hilly, urban city. In 2010, skateboarders started using a stretch of Waller Street that had been closed to traffic. The skateboarding community took care of the space and each other, winning over the neighborhood and the city government. In partnership with the skateboarding community, San Francisco Recreation & Parks made this an official skate park in 2022 and added a suite of street-style features and smooth-coated asphalt. It was renamed for Zion Williams-Gaines, a San Franciscan skateboarder and community advocate who died in 2023.

5 **Ride the vintage 1912 carousel.** When you ride the carousel, look in the center to spot a horse like one from the park's original carousel from the 1890s. Then look up to the paintings on the sides of the carousel for scenes from yesteryear in the park.

WHAT TO KNOW: This spacious skate park is always open and not too crowded. All ages and skill levels are found here, including younger kids taking classes.

Soccer

LOCATION: Beach Chalet Athletic Fields at 1500 JFK Drive (plus other fields)

It's unknown exactly when people started playing soccer in the park, but the city has a surprisingly long history with it. The San Francisco Soccer Football League dates back to 1902. When baseball fields were built in 1933 where the current Beach Chalet Athletic Fields are, people likely started playing soccer there, too. By the early 1940s, historical photos show soccer goals and games on the grounds. Over the decades, baseball faded out and the Beach Chalet Athletic Fields became *the* place for soccer in the park, with a complete renovation in 2015 adding synthetic turf and lights to accommodate many more games on the four regulation fields.

WHAT TO KNOW: The Beach Chalet Athletic Fields are in very high demand by clubs and programs. However, you'd be surprised how quiet the fields can be on summer evenings. If a field is open, feel free to kick around a ball with the sound of the Pacific Ocean and the Murphy Windmill in the background. Pitch 1C/D is also kept

Although the Beach Chalet Athletic Fields are often booked solid by soccer clubs and programs, one pitch is kept available for open play much of the time.

available for open play Monday through Friday from 9 a.m. to 3 p.m., Tuesday and Thursday from 7:30 p.m. to 9 p.m., and Sunday from 9 a.m. to 11 a.m. On Sunday from 11 a.m. to 1 p.m., it's open play for kids fourteen and under.

The Beach Chalet Athletic Fields aren't the only place soccer is played in the park. The Polo Field and Little Rec Field can only be reserved for leagues; the Polo Field is otherwise locked. You can make a single reservation for field space at Beach Chalet for playing with friends and family two weeks in advance (leagues and programs must do advanced reservations for a season). While most of the soccer played in the park is with organized leagues, there are casual, coed pick-up games to be found online and sometimes at Big Rec Ball Field. If you're just looking to kick around a ball for a bit, Robin Williams Meadow is a nice, flat spot. Pro tip: you can watch professional soccer at Kezar Stadium. It's now the home of the new Golden City Football Club.

Ultimate Frisbee

LOCATION: Various spots

Ultimate frisbee, which started taking off in the 1970s, can be played in many parts of the park at any time. Games (league and pick-up) are usually played at the Polo Field, Beach Chalet Athletic Fields, or Big Rec Ball Field.

WHAT TO KNOW: The Bay Area Disc Association organizes leagues; learn more at bayareadisc.org. You can find pick-up game opportunities at https://pickup ultimate.com. There's also Big Gay Frisbee, a queer recreational ultimate frisbee league. Learn more at bgfsanfrancisco.com.

Volleyball

LOCATION: Often found in Peacock Meadow and the lawn area near where Kezar Drive and JFK Promenade intersect, plus Upper Big Rec Fields

While there are no permanent volleyball courts in the park, lawns on the far eastern end of the park are often used for pick-up games on the grass. Sometimes people even set up portable lights to extend playtime in the evenings. Some fields (including Peacock Meadow) are closed every other month to allow the turf to recover.

WHAT TO KNOW: Wednesdays, Saturdays, and Sundays (or any day the weather's notably warm) are when you're most likely to find people playing. As of publication, the Heylo app is the only way to sign up for specific pick-up games in the park. Games range from casual to competitive, but some basic skills are expected. Showing up and asking to join in is generally welcomed. There are also recreational leagues that play in the park; check out volosports.com.

Yoga, Zumba, and More

WHAT TO KNOW: Yoga is regularly offered at the Botanical Garden and at the Conservatory of Flowers; check the calendar at gggp.org. Private instructors also hold classes throughout the park; a quick internet search will point you toward

Heroes of the Park: All Staff and Volunteer Gardeners

When you look at what the park started as and what it became, it's almost all thanks to gardeners. William Hammond Hall, who designed the park and then oversaw it during the first five years, wasn't a gardener. But he *was* an engineer. He applied his problem-solving mindset to turn sand into soil and quickly get sizable trees growing, and he essentially became a gardener. Hall then did something crucial: he recommended that John McLaren, a master gardener, be hired as the park's assistant superintendent in 1887. What a hire that proved to be, especially once McLaren was promoted to superintendent in 1890.

McLaren was obsessed with bringing a diversity of plants, trees, and flowers to the park and making it a showplace of nature's beauty. McLaren and everyone who worked for him over the next half a century nurtured the ultimate public garden.

Countless gardeners, both staff and volunteers, have built on this while also evolving the park in ways McLaren would approve of. Today, gardeners incorporate more native plants and remove problematic non-native species to reduce water use and to support birds, butterflies, and bugs. They also bring their artistry to everything from the flower beds in front of the Conservatory of Flowers to delightful little-known areas on the west side.

And big props to all the volunteers. The Dahlia Dell is 100 percent volunteer-led. Fuchsia Dell was restored a few years ago mostly by volunteers, who now maintain the area every Friday morning. The creation of the National AIDS Memorial Grove was a significant undertaking made possible because of volunteers (see p. 86). Volunteers continue to donate around 4,500 hours of work a year!

these. Free Zumba classes are regularly offered by San Francisco Recreation & Parks near the carousel. Go to sfrecpark.org for a current schedule. You'll also find other activities in the park—everything from slacklining and sound baths to tai chi and qigong. Read more on p. 105 about how to find activities.

Volunteering

Volunteering is a great way to give back to the park and keep the golden era of Golden Gate Park going strong. The most direct way to jump into volunteering is through the San Francisco Recreation & Parks volunteer calendar. Go to sfrecpark.org/1665/Park-Volunteers, click on "Volunteer Calendar," and then search in "District 1." You'll typically find several options in the park within the next month, including habitat restoration and gardening projects at a range of locations. You do need to sign up to participate; don't just show up. During Earth Month (April), San Francisco Recreation & Parks lists even more volunteer opportunities at sfrecpark.org.

There are work days on the third Sunday of each month at the National AIDS Memorial Grove (details at aidsmemorial.org), and you can help out at the Dahlia Dell if you're a member of the San Francisco Dahlia Society (learn more at dahliadell.org). There are also many volunteer opportunities within the **Gardens of Golden Gate Park** (which includes the Conservatory of Flowers, the Japanese Tea Garden, and the Botanical Garden). You can help with plant sales, special events like Flower Piano, office support, becoming an interpretive guide, and more. However, you do need to complete an online orientation, get a background check, and potentially have additional training, depending on the role. Go to gggp.org/volunteer to learn more and sign up for the program.

There's also a wide range of volunteer opportunities at the **de Young Museum** and **California Academy of Sciences**. These are generally longer-term commitments with additional requirements. You can even be a volunteer diver in the Philippine coral reef tank at the Academy of Sciences and clean the tank and feed the fish!

Love JFK Promenade? There are a variety of ways to help year-round, often involving the art installations or events led by local nonprofit Illuminate. Fill out the volunteer interest form at illuminate.org to get emails with upcoming opportunities.

THE WILD SIDE: FINDING NATURE IN THE PARK

Since the start, the vision for the park was centered on connecting with nature, which can be experienced in a remarkable number of forms in this one place. You can soak up the quiet of a 100-year-old redwood forest or spot a bird that's migrated from halfway around the world. You can see rare and endangered plants and animals from some of the remotest parts of the planet, or watch an American bison munch on grass while a great blue heron hunts gophers nearby. Get out there!

Opposite: ***Near the Bison Paddock, habitat has been restored to support the endangered Nuttall's white-crowned sparrow.***
(Photo by Eddie Bartley)

Before the park was built, what was called the "Great Sand Bank" wasn't the wasteland many proclaimed it to be. It was home to a range of habitats: coastal dune scrub, coastal dune, grasslands, and coast live oak woodlands. There were small freshwater lakes, ponds, and wetlands scattered around. And many birds, mammals, and insects were uniquely dependent on these habitats. While the park's creation wiped out a lot of this ecological diversity, all was not lost—and some things were gained in surprising ways.

First, the **coast live oak woodlands** in the northeastern corner of the park were preserved. Perhaps in William Hammond Hall's desperation to get trees in the park, he figured he should keep the ones already growing. These woodlands are a biodiversity hotspot within the park (more on p. 148).

Coastal dune scrub habitat, which has dense shrubs mixed with grasses, wildflowers, and open sand on inland dunes, was largely destroyed in the park and throughout the San Francisco Peninsula. In the 1940s, this led to the first known insect extinction from human causes: the loss of the Xerces blue butterfly. But

The coast live oak woodlands in the northeastern corner of the park represent one of the park's native ecosystems.

the park has been planting more and more native coastal scrub plants, which are crucial to support species like the endangered Nuttall's white-crowned sparrow (see p. 139). You'll see plenty of sticky monkeyflower and bush lupine in the park; both plants are native to coastal dune scrub habitat. To experience a remnant of coastal scrub habitat, head to the Balboa Natural Area at Balboa Street and the Great Highway (just a couple of blocks from the western edge of the park).

Coastal dune habitat is what's between the dune scrub habitat and the ocean itself, with sparse and low shrubs and other vegetation like dune grass and beach strawberries (these days you see a lot of non-native ice plants, too). You can experience this habitat along Ocean Beach. There is no **coastal grassland** habitat left in San Francisco, and little left statewide, but Point Reyes National Seashore is one place to experience it. Today's Golden Gate Park does have something it didn't historically have: several **coastal redwood groves** (more on p. 149). The California coast is the only place in the world where these redwoods grow; they love the fog, so these trees are doing well in the park.

There's another piece to the story of the park when it comes to preserving biodiversity. San Francisco's cool, foggy climate allows gardeners at the Botanical Garden to grow highly endangered plants from high-elevation African and South American cloud forests that face climate change and deforestation. The California Academy of Sciences shows people the wonders of a living Philippine coral reef while also doing cutting-edge research to save reefs in the age of warming oceans. The Conservatory of Flowers is home to more than thirty plant species that are globally endangered or critically endangered. And, of course, there's the remarkable diversity of birds in the park (more below), which wouldn't have been as rich without all the park's trees. Meanwhile, the park is increasingly using native species for new plantings, and it now uses 100 percent recycled water.

Birds and Birding

An incredible number of birds make Golden Gate Park their home throughout the seasons. The park was described as a "great outdoor aviary" by Joseph Mailliard in his 1930 book *The Birds of Golden Gate Park*. Indeed! Over the years, over two hundred species of resident and migratory birds have been seen in the park.

Great blue herons, red-tailed hawks, California scrub jays, Steller's jays, California towhees, dark-eyed juncos, brown creepers, western bluebirds, Anna's hummingbirds, pygmy nuthatches, downy woodpeckers, American robins, and black phoebes are frequently seen, easy to identify, and do not migrate. These birds also are accustomed to being around people, so you'll often get to observe them from a close distance. Many more species pass through while migrating. As a tree-filled oasis right along the Pacific Flyway—one of the major north-south routes that hundreds of species of birds use each year—the park offers a resting place, water, and food on long journeys. It's why birders have spotted the tropical yellow-green vireo and even a rare rustic bunting from Asia in the park.

Birding with the Golden Gate Bird Alliance

For more than twenty years, Golden Gate Bird Alliance has offered free birding walks on the first Sunday of the month at 8 a.m. with knowledgeable birders in the Botanical Garden. This is a welcoming space for birders of all experience levels, including first-timers. Guides take you around the garden, helping you hear and spot different species. No bird is considered too common! This birding community is excited to welcome newcomers and help ensure that you spot special birds in particular. Bring binoculars and be prepared to be out for three to four hours in what often starts as very chilly weather. RSVPs are appreciated so there are enough guides. Registration opens a week before-hand and is through the Gardens of Golden Gate Park at gggp.org/events-calendar. Learn more about the Golden Gate Bird Alliance at goldengatebirdalliance.org.

Want to know when a rare bird has been spotted? Go to ebird.org and sign up for alerts for San Francisco County. At ebird.org, go to "Explore" and enter "San Francisco," and you can zoom in on Golden Gate Park and find lists of species found at various locations in the park. At sfbirds.net, you can get direct links to recent San Francisco bird sightings lists that include rare birds (and join the alert list). If you go to inaturalist.org and search for "birds of Golden Gate Park," you'll get a quick view (with photos) of the most common species seen, plus the most recent sightings by users. The Merlin app from Cornell Labs is also great for identifying birds by song or sight.

Best Times of Year for Birding

Birding, which has been popular since the park's inception, is excellent year-round in the park. But there are seasons to birding, because while some species are year-round residents, many others are migratory.

If you hike up and directly along Huntington Falls on Strawberry Hill, you may see Anna's hummingbirds bathing near the top. *(Photo by Robert Ho)*

The spring migration is February through May, and the fall migration is August through November. Birders say that May, August, and September have extra-high numbers of migrating birds. Some migratory birds will stay a while, like Townsend's warblers, which winter here. There are also birds that summer in San Francisco (despite the cool weather), like Wilson's warblers, Swainson's thrushes, and hooded orioles.

Of course, springtime (in San Francisco from about February to May) is when many baby birds hatch. If you want a high likelihood of spotting baby birds, head to Blue Heron Lake to see the heron chicks (more on these below), ducklings, and goslings. Great horned owls usually nest somewhere in the park, with word of owlets spreading among birders and photographers. Early morning and dusk are prime times for birding. The quiet of early morning allows you to hear more bird calls, and dusk is when many birds are out catching insects.

Best Places to Go Birding

The Botanical Garden is the top hotspot for birding in the park. The various plants, flowers, and trees provide plenty of food and shelter for birds. The Botanical Garden always opens at 7:30 a.m., which is a great time for birding, plus everyone gets in free before 9 a.m. (more on p. 75).

Birders have favorite trees and locations within the Botanical Garden. The Children's Garden has a hidden pond where you can see purple finches, many types of warblers, and sometimes an unusual bird. Check out the huge Guatemalan fir tree in the open meadow by the Redwood Grove; it's especially popular with warblers and golden-crowned kinglets.

The other birdiest parts of the park include North Lake, Middle Lake, and Blue Heron Lake. Blue Heron Lake always has a range of ducks, including some anomalies like domestic Muscovy ducks that were likely left here by previous pet owners (as were many of the turtles you see resting on logs). There are typically wild mallards, wood ducks, double-crested cormorants, hooded mergansers, buffleheads, and a variety of gulls. Strawberry Hill, in the center of Blue Heron Lake, is where you'll find migrating and wintering warblers, nuthatches, and vireos.

Birds of Note

Great blue herons have become one of the park's most iconic species in recent years. This is partly because they're hard to miss: these leggy, long-necked birds are more than four feet tall. Great blue herons are also visible because they're in almost every part of the park, often in plain sight on lawns and open fields. These clever birds don't just hunt in ponds and lakes like you'd expect; they are adept at hunting for underground pocket gophers (which park gardeners will tell you there's no shortage of). The heron's curved neck and beak can strike out to stab prey at 90 miles per hour!

While great blue herons have always been present in the park, they only started nesting here in 1993. Over the years, the tall trees in the islands of Blue Heron Lake have proven ideal for the birds, with several pairs now typically nesting here and hundreds of chicks hatched over the years. You will start to see activity in the trees in January, when courtship behaviors begin. Once a pair has bonded for the season, the male goes off searching for sticks and the female decides if his findings are good enough to use for an existing nest or a new one. By mid-March, the females usually lay two to five eggs, and the parents trade off sitting on the nest for about a month. By mid-April, chicks are hatching and the parents begin their relentless hunting to feed the very fast-growing babies (listen for the hangry squawks of the chicks). After about eight weeks, chicks are stretching their wings and hopping around, readying for their first flights. Chicks fledge at twelve weeks. While it's nice to have binoculars, the birds are easily observed without them, thanks to their size and the size of the stick nests.

Golden Gate Park played a major role in bringing the American bison back from the brink of extinction (more on p. 144). So it's fitting that today the bison paddock is part of important work to protect another endangered species: the **Nuttall's white-crowned sparrow**. Nuttall's white-crowned sparrows are a subspecies of white-crowned sparrow; they only live near the California coast, have their own unique song, do not migrate, and were once abundant in the region. But over the decades, as has been the case for many bird species, their habitat has been whittled down to scraps. Nuttall's white-crowned sparrows need open fields to forage in, some tall grass for hiding, and a mix of shrub types nearby for breeding.

The leggy great blue herons and their chicks become minor celebrities in spring. Tracking them through the breeding season is entertaining if you're local. *(Photo by Robert Ho)*

The bison paddock has the "open fields" part covered. In 2009, native coastal dune species were planted on the hillside in front of the paddock, including sticky monkeyflower, California bee plant, coast buckwheat, and yellow bush lupine. This is what would have been here before the park was built. Note that the birdhouses you see along the bison paddock are for western bluebirds and tree swallows. Volunteers help maintain this area once a month; you can join them (more on p. 131)!

Despite being the official bird of San Francisco and the state itself, the last **California quail** was seen in the park in 2018. While these birds are not endangered, many parkgoers grieved the loss of this charismatic bird with its trademark plume. Because it's a ground-dwelling bird that's not great at flying, domestic cats, raccoons, and vehicle traffic are primarily to blame for its disappearance. Sufficient underbrush and shrubbery are also key for quail, and their preferred coastal scrub habitat is limited in the park.

One of the best things about the park is how you can feel far from the city surrounding you and even experience a sense of true wildness. The **red-tailed hawk** adds a lot to this feeling. Red-tailed hawks are a common sight soaring above the

A Hero of the Park: Nancy DeStefanis

On a spring day in 1993, Nancy DeStefanis was on a walk around what's now called Blue Heron Lake when she spotted a heron flying down into a tall Monterey pine tree. The heron landed on what had to be a nest. It was a big moment for both the birds and DeStefanis: the herons had found what would prove to be successful nesting grounds for generations of chicks, while DeStefanis found her calling as an ambassador for the birds.

For over thirty years, DeStefanis and the organization she founded, San Francisco Nature Education, has led a program on Saturdays in the spring for the public to learn about the herons and spot their large-and-in-charge babies, using high-powered scopes. Learn more at sfnature.org. DeStefanis has connected tens of thousands of people, especially kids, with the wonders of nature. When Stow Lake was being renamed in 2023, DeStefanis passionately and successfully rallied support for the name Blue Heron Lake, a perfect choice that reminds us to always look up into the trees.

park or perched high in trees, and the bird's piercing "keeeee-arrr" cry is transporting. During flight, the light shining through its rusty-colored tail feathers makes it pretty easy to identify. Keep an eye out for a pale chest and dark wingtips as well when identifying this bird of prey. Red-tailed hawks nest in the park, which means spring brings extra sightings of juveniles. There are also aggressive air shows between the hawks and ravens, with these two species defending territories and nests. Red-tailed, red-shouldered, and Cooper's are the three hawk species regularly found in the park.

Support Birds in Your Backyard by Creating Insect-Friendly Habitat

Nearly all North American bird species depend on insects as part of their diet for at least part of their life cycle. But insect populations are dropping precipitously due to habitat loss and pesticides. This is bad news for birds, but you can help by planting native plants, leaving leaf litter for insects, and avoiding pesticides in your yard (and at the grocery store by buying organic).

Butterflies

The park attracts more than a dozen butterfly species and provides many nectaring flowers for butterflies to eat. At least a few species of butterflies are around every month of the year, with April and September peak months for many species. The best place to look for butterflies is the park's highest peak, Strawberry Hill in Blue Heron Lake, on nice days (they don't like cold and wind). Butterflies seek out hills to find one another in a behavior called "hilltopping." Species most commonly seen in the park include American and West Coast ladies, anise swallowtails, red admirals, painted and common checkered skippers, and monarchs.

The California pipevine swallowtail butterfly is only found where its namesake native plant is. In the park, look for it in the Botanical Garden and on Strawberry Hill. *(Photo by Liam O'Brien)*

The park plays host to one of the most stunning butterflies in North

America: the California pipevine swallowtail. When it's a caterpillar, the California pipevine swallowtail will only feed on the California pipevine plant. Unfortunately, as this native plant became rare in the city, so did the butterfly (which thankfully isn't endangered as a species). But Golden Gate Park is bucking this trend in two places where lots of pipevine has been planted: on Strawberry Hill in Blue Heron Lake and in the California natives area in the Botanical Garden (look right in front of the fenced-off pond by the nursery). You'll see the pipevine swallowtails from March through June, both as large black caterpillars with orange spikes and as adult winged beauties.

If you want guaranteed butterfly sightings, head to the Osher Rainforest in the California Academy of Sciences, where tropical species transported weekly from Costa Rica will flutter around you. The Living Roof at the California Academy of Sciences is also a hotspot for butterflies; it's planted with native annuals and perennials specifically to support several species. You can support butterflies by volunteering to restore butterfly habitat on Strawberry Hill on the second Saturday morning of each month. Creating a butterfly garden with native flowering plants is wonderful, and if you're local, include some California pipevine, which is available at many nurseries in the city.

Spiders

One of nature's most spectacular spiders spins its intricate, wheel-shaped webs in the park. Orb-weaver spiders are easy to find once you know where to look—and they're fascinating to observe. There are many species of orb-weavers, but the ones you'll most often find in the park have banded legs and large, patterned abdomens and are about three-fourths of an inch across. After finding a good space, these hardworking engineers build a sturdy frame of silk and then add spokes of a stretchy capture thread with sticky droplets. If you want to be stunned by what these spiders do, look up "Beautiful Spider Web Build Time-lapse | BBC Earth" on YouTube.

Ready for your own spidering adventures? Then head to the plants and shrubs in front of the Conservatory of Flowers, on the paths near Lily Pond, and the eastern edge of the Music Concourse. The spiders especially like the lily of the Nile plants. They are most active and visible in the early morning, and morning dew makes their webs really stand out. Dusk is also a good time to look for them. The orb-weaver spiders don't have a fixed season in the Bay Area climate, but you can

If you think you've seen it all in the park, try spidering. *(Photo by Megan Taylor)*

spot them most abundantly from August to October. Fall is also when you may see some messy webs spun to hold egg sacs. You can follow them as they take down and rebuild their daily orb web to capture flying insects, and if you're lucky, you might spot a male playing a female a song by lightly strumming the silk strands on the edge of her web.

Orb-weaver spiders are harmless and provide a great service to humans by keeping insect populations in check. Don't disturb these remarkable park dwellers. There are nearly two hundred kinds of orb-weavers in North America, but the ones seen in the park are usually the cross orb-weaver, the shamrock orb-weaver, and the six-spotted orb-weaver.

Notable Animals Then and Now

A friend once marveled to me about the fact that a major city like San Francisco has a herd of bison grazing in a park. It *is* remarkable, as are the stories of how bison and coyotes came to be here and how grizzly bears came and went.

Coyotes: A Top Predator Is Back

Despite being native to San Francisco, coyotes became locally extinct about a century ago. The last coyote in all of San Francisco was reportedly seen in Golden Gate

Coyotes have made a comeback in San Francisco and the park after being locally extinct. *(Photo by Robert Ho)*

Park in 1925. Coyotes departed as the city was being built up and automobiles arrived, but people also poisoned and hunted coyotes, driving their numbers to zero. However, in the early 2000s, people started to spot coyotes in the city's biggest green spaces: the Presidio, McLaren Park, and Golden Gate Park. DNA tests showed these coyotes were related to ones up north, which means they got here via the Golden Gate Bridge!

These adaptable, intelligent members of the dog family love eating rodents and have done well since their comeback. San Francisco's "live and let live" ethos is now applied to this top predator, with coyotes being monitored and managed rather than exterminated. They are part of the ecosystem, after all. And seeing one in the park is a true moment of beauty and wildness, like hearing the piercing cry of a red-tailed hawk.

March through September is pupping season for coyotes. This means they can get protective, so people with dogs should be extra aware, steer clear, and be sure dogs are leashed. Coyotes are more active in the early morning and evening. If a coyote is acting abnormally, call San Francisco Animal Care and Control at (415) 554-9400. Never feed coyotes or leave food trash behind. Let's keep coyotes healthy and wild!

The Remarkable Story of the Park's Bison

When you first learn there is a herd of American bison living in the park, it may seem a little odd. And it *is* strange, given that modern bison were never even in California, though some prehistoric bison did live in the state. American bison, also sometimes called buffalo, were first brought to the park in 1891. At the time, these creatures fit in with the park's wild—and Wild West—feel. Kangaroos, emus, grizzly bears, moose, sheep, and goats were also brought to the park around then.

Bison, however, were on the brink of extinction in the wild, largely due to mass slaughter by white colonists (including the US Army). Their numbers were down to less than a thousand from tens of *millions*. Thankfully, national conservation efforts began just in time to prevent the loss of bison forever. In the park, bison breeding was so successful that offspring from the park's herd were used to help restock wild herds. Today, American bison are at a stable "near threatened" conservation level as a species, and many even exist in wild, free-roaming herds in other parts of the country. The park now only has female bison in order to keep the herd small. Speaking of free-roaming, twenty-five bison escaped from the park into the nearby Richmond and Sunset neighborhoods in 1925!

The bison paddock is located at 1237 JFK Drive on the western end of the park. The bison are almost always on view for the public, though sometimes you may

American bison have been in the park since 1891, and successful breeding here played a role in preventing their extinction in the United States. *(Photo by Jim Watkins)*

need to walk around the back of their paddock to spot them. The only time the bison aren't out in the pasture is during feeding time. Feeding time happens around their enclosure between 11 a.m. and 1 p.m. each day, which makes it a good time to see them from a much closer spot than many parts of the paddock. Staff from the San Francisco Zoo care for the bison.

Grizzly Bears and a Bear Named Monarch

Up until the Gold Rush, there were an estimated 10,000 grizzly bears throughout California. But by the time a grizzly bear named Monarch ended up in Golden Gate Park in 1894, the California grizzly was all but extinct due to hunting by white colonists. William Randolph Hearst, the wealthy owner of the *San Francisco Examiner*, wanted to sell more newspapers, so he paid for the search and capture of one of the state's last grizzlies as a publicity stunt. In 1889, a grizzly that Hearst named Monarch was trapped in the San Gabriel Mountains and brought to San Francisco.

Monarch made big news and became a wildly popular attraction at Woodward's Garden, a "public amusement resort" in the city. Five years later, Monarch was moved into Golden Gate Park. He was put in a large cage where park visitors could go right up to the bars and even throw in food. A female grizzly was added in 1903, and the pair had cubs. After seventeen years in the park, Monarch died in 1911, but the "Bear Pit" remained until 1939. By then, grizzly bears were extinct in California, with the last sighting in 1924.

The sad, strange tale of Monarch is worth reflecting on. Monarch's stuffed pelt is sometimes on display at the California Academy of Sciences. You can also visit where Monarch lived in the oak woodlands just west of the National AIDS Memorial Grove. Monarch reminds us of how quickly a species can be lost—and what we lose as a result.

Trees of Golden Gate Park

More than anything else, trees make Golden Gate Park what it is: trees of all sizes and species, creating canopies above our heads, filtering the light and framing the meadows, blocking the Pacific winds, and providing habitat for birds and bugs. Trees are why and how the park feels like a true retreat into nature.

But before Golden Gate Park was created, it was nearly treeless except for the coast live oaks in the northeastern corner of the park. What tree could take root in

The main ingredient in the park's beauty and wildness is its abundance of large trees, like the ones on Blue Heron Island.

constantly shifting sand dunes? Frederick Law Olmsted had deemed it impossible. William Hammond Hall proved him wrong, and John McLaren then built on Hall's success with wild tree-planting abandon. As mentioned earlier in this book, Hall quickly found three tree species that would grow quickly into a canopy: Monterey pine, Monterey cypress, and blue gum eucalyptus. But once these were in place to provide shelter for young plants, McLaren began planting all kinds of trees. The vast majority were evergreen.

Aerial photos of the eastern half of the park in 1894 show a remarkable number of good-sized trees already, with full tree cover on much of the land. By 1895, the park had planted 825 different types of trees. The park was barely twenty-five years old! Today there are an estimated 130,000 trees in the park, representing every corner of the planet. The Botanical Garden alone has nearly two hundred species of trees. The park is a living tree museum.

What you won't find in the park are many hardwood tree species native to the East Coast of the United States. They won't grow here; many of those trees need cold winters. But who needs 'em? You'll find the oldest trees in the park in two areas: the Panhandle, which was the first part of the park to be planted, and the coast live oak woodlands in the far northeastern corner, which is a native forest (more on this below).

Coast Live Oak Woodlands

In the northeastern corner of the park are fifty acres of forest that will transport you back in time to before there was a park or even a San Francisco. Welcome to the coast live oak woodlands, with curving branches, abundant acorns, and more biodiversity than any other land ecosystem type in California. Coast live oak woodlands thrive in the foggy coastal areas in California and were historically a key food source for Indigenous people. The coast live oak is the only tree native to San Francisco. The oak woodlands in the park are the oldest, largest remnant of this native habitat in the city, and the area is a designated old-growth forest. (Some trees have been harvested, likely after the 1906 earthquake and during the Gold Rush years, but it's been untouched for more than a century now.)

The park's oak woodland is a healthy ecosystem teeming with life. There's a "Golden Gate Park Oak Woodlands Checklist" at inaturalist.org that shows all the flora and fauna you will find. Look for the adorable chestnut-backed chickadee, which nests in cavities in coast live oaks and lives here year-round. Or keep an eye and ear out for one of four types of woodpeckers found in the oak woodlands: downy, hairy, acorn, and Nuttall's. The trees with small, red berries and leathery leaves are toyon, commonly found in oak woodland ecosystems.

The 0.8-mile, mostly unpaved **Phil Arnold Trail** is the main trail through the oak woodlands and is highly recommended, especially in spring. The primary trailhead is near McLaren Lodge, located at the corner of JFK Promenade and Conservatory Drive East, but you can get on the trail from many locations. Note that this is a multiuse trail, so you may see mountain bikers. The Phil Arnold Trail is part of the **Bay Area Ridge Trail**, a project to encircle the region with one connected trail system. Phil Arnold led the completion of the Bay Area Ridge Trail segment in San Francisco; he was a public servant for San Francisco for more than thirty years and a champion for parks and open space until his death in 2019. Another true hero of the park!

You will find coast live oaks throughout the park. There's a small oak woodland with accessible paths next to the Haight Street entrance. And at the far western end of the National AIDS Memorial Grove is a delightful oak woodland full of monastery stones (more on p. 183).

Redwood Trees

There's nothing like the feeling of being surrounded by redwood trees. Happily, there are hundreds of California coastal redwoods (*Sequoia sempervirens*) in the park, including several groves. The fog-loving coastal redwoods are the tallest trees in the world and can live to be more than 2,000 years old. The coastal redwoods in the park were all planted after the park's creation, so they are young in the grand scheme of their species. But many are old enough to have trunks taller than one hundred feet. I like to imagine them towering over the park when it celebrates its 250th or 500th birthday.

The five best coastal redwood groves are in Fuchsia Dell, the National AIDS Memorial Grove, Redwood Memorial Grove off of JFK Promenade, Heroes Grove off of JFK Promenade, and the Redwood Grove in the Botanical Garden. Note that there is a redwood with albino offshoots in the Botanical Garden's grove—see if you can find these rare, ghostly babies at the base of one of the redwoods! Visiting these groves makes for a great walk in the eastern half of the park.

What about California's *other* world-famous redwood and the world's largest tree: the giant sequoia (*Sequoiadendron giganteum*)? You can find these in the park, too, though not in groves. The oldest giant sequoia in the park is likely the

What's Up with the Trees in the Music Concourse?

When recently pollarded or bare of leaves, the trees in the Music Concourse look very strange. *(Photo by Jim Watkins)*

Researching this book led me to some new vocabulary, including the word "pollarding." Pollarding is how the trees in the Music Concourse are pruned, basically by flat-topping them once a year. The Music Concourse trees look pretty skeletal and strange if you see them right after pollarding. But as the branches grow and the leaves sprout, it creates a charming continuous canopy that is very European. The majority of the trees in the Music Concourse are London plane and Scotch elm trees.

one you'll find near the corner of Conservatory Drive West and JFK Promenade, planted in 1894. It is the centerpiece of the wooded area; look for a plaque on a large stone near the trunk.

The Janis Joplin Tree

At the base of Hippie Hill in Robin Williams Meadow, you'll find a shaggy elm tree along the path leading away from the hill. It's under this tree that singer-songwriter and 1960s rock icon Janis Joplin is said to have played guitar. Joplin lived nearby in the Haight-Ashbury neighborhood, and as the counterculture movement grew, Hippie Hill became an extension of the neighborhood.

This shaggy elm tree at the base of Hippie Hill is where singer-songwriter and 1960s rock icon Janis Joplin would play her guitar. *(Photo by Nancy Botkin)*

Monterey Cypresses and Uncle John's Tree

Probably the most iconic tree of the park is the Monterey cypress, which grows exclusively on the Monterey Peninsula, a little more than a hundred miles south of San Francisco. The Monterey cypress was an early favorite to plant in the park because these trees love the coastal fog and make great windbreaks. The ocean winds give these trees their distinctive flat-topped look that makes them easy to identify from a distance, especially on the western end of the park.

Many Monterey cypresses tower above the park, and a few of the giants are well-known and loved: the cypress on the Great Meadow at the Botanical Garden, the cypress leaning next to JFK Promenade behind the de Young Museum, and the cypress known as "Uncle John's Tree." Named for John McLaren, this tree, which was planted in the earliest years of the park, is over a hundred feet tall and likely over 130 years old. It was there when McLaren lived in the lodge, and I imagine he looked at it often over the years as it grew to impressive heights. Each December, the tree is adorned with a thousand lights, and a tree-lighting event is held for the entire city. It's the city's official holiday tree! During the Great Depression, McLaren

The towering Monterey cypress on JFK Promenade near the de Young Museum is worth a visit and dates back to the park's early years.

started this tradition to bring some joy to the children (and also maybe because he was appointed to the Outdoor Christmas Tree Association of California). With McLaren's birthday on December 20, it's fitting that the city continues to remember him at this time each year.

Eucalyptus Trees

As William Hammond Hall hurried to get good-sized trees growing in the park, he found a boon in eucalypts. Free from all their native pests back in Australia and New

Zealand, nothing seemed to stop these trees from growing *fast*: three to four feet a year. The blue gum is one of the tallest kinds of eucalyptus, growing more than one hundred feet tall even in poor soil. There are very large blue gum eucalyptus trees throughout the park. They are easy to identify by their peeling bark and long, thin leaves redolent with fragrant oil. They're so numerous throughout California that many people (like me when I first moved here) assume they're native and even think they "smell like California."

There are around fifty species of eucalypts (woody Australian plants belonging to several related genera, including *Eucalyptus*) in the park, totaling thousands of trees. But as the eucalypts die, the park is opting to replace them with native California trees like Monterey pines, Monterey cypress, coast live oaks, coastal redwoods, and Torrey pines. Fun fact: The San Francisco Zoo harvests fresh eucalyptus leaves from trees around the city to feed the koalas, including about 5 percent from the park.

A Hero of the Park: Elizabeth McClintock

"Anybody could have done it. It just turns out that I was the one," said Elizabeth McClintock (1912–2004). McClintock, a renowned botanist, spent years identifying and documenting much of the park's tree diversity, which was vital for managing the vast and complex urban forest. She also created the first plant-record system for the Botanical Garden. McClintock did all this for the pure love of it.

McClintock worked for thirty years at the California Academy of Sciences, where she was crucial in preserving the collection of California native flora. Outside the Academy's doors, she was a passionate advocate for protecting nature. One way she did this was as part of the campaign to prevent the Panhandle from becoming an eight-lane freeway. McClintock created a booklet detailing every one of the Panhandle's trees to show exactly what would be lost: about two hundred ecologically important leafy friends. Her out-of-print book, *The Trees of Golden Gate Park and San Francisco*, is a treasure featuring detailed maps, stories, and information on over 170 types of trees found in the park.

California poppies, a native flower, are popping in the park most of the year. But the flower cup only opens when it's sunny. *(Photo by Jim Watkins)*

All Abloom: When and Where to See Flowers

John McLaren wasn't just all about the trees—his botanical obsession included flowers, too. McLaren wanted a park where you could enjoy blooms year-round. He succeeded, as any walk in the park will show you, especially in the Botanical Garden. There are some especially spectacular flowers to catch at certain times of year.

Calla lilies: January to June. It's often right after the New Year when you start to see these popping up around the park as a sign of San Francisco's springtime. Hotspots are around all the lakes and anywhere with soggier ground.

Magnolias: January to March. The Botanical Garden has more than two hundred beauties, including many rare and endangered species. When they blossom at the start of the year, it's a social-media sensation. You'll find magnolias throughout the park, too.

California golden poppies: February to September. You'll find California's official flower throughout the park. But the cups only open when the sun is shining!

Tulips: March to April. Ten thousand of these bloom at the Queen Wilhelmina Garden at the Dutch Windmill. The garden was planted and named in 1962 to honor Wilhelmina Helena Pauline Maria, who was queen of the Netherlands for fifty-eight years (the longest-reigning monarch in Dutch history).

Cherry blossoms (sakura): March to April. These are especially abundant in the Japanese Tea Garden, but you'll also find them in the Botanical Garden, around Blue Heron Lake, and scattered elsewhere in the park.

Rhododendrons: April to May. Not only is there John McLaren Memorial Rhododendron Dell, there's also a Rhododendron Garden tucked away in the Botanical Garden. Together, these include hundreds of varieties of McLaren's favorite flower.

Cherry blossoms, or sakura, are stunning in spring. While the Japanese Tea Garden has many, you'll find them elsewhere, like this flowering cherry tree near Blue Heron Lake.

From May through November, be sure to check out San Francisco's official flower in Dahlia Dell. *(Photo by Jim Watkins)*

Roses: Mid-May to July, plus September and a few varieties even in December. Head to the Rose Garden on JFK Promenade for an impressive number of rose varieties. The garden's location was carefully chosen and oriented to protect the roses from the wind and catch the most rays, given the park's cool temperatures and fog.

Dahlias: June to November. Find these at the Dahlia Dell next to the Conservatory of Flowers. Dahlias were chosen as the official flower of San Francisco in 1926 because, thanks to their beauty and diversity, they are the "very symbol of San Francisco life and of the spirit of her people." The peak of dahlia season is late August. Learn more on p. 84.

Fuchsias: May to November. Find more of these delicate blossoms than you can imagine in Fuchsia Dell in the northeastern corner of the park. This hidden gem has been lovingly restored in recent years thanks to many volunteers.

Fall foliage: Late September to early December; peak is late November. There aren't many deciduous trees in San Francisco that showcase the yellow, orange, and red leaves of fall. But you can find spots for leaf peeping in Golden Gate Park, especially if you go in search of Japanese maple and ginkgo trees. The Japanese Tea Garden and the Botanical Garden (especially the Moon Viewing Garden) are your best bets. JFK Promenade also has some golden beauties on the Golden Mile, especially near the Pioneer Log Cabin.

WALKS AND HIKES

There's no better way to get to know the park's many sides than on foot and off the beaten path. This book includes eleven walks and hikes of varying lengths and difficulties; all highlight lesser-known spots and stories. Whether you walk in the footsteps of giants like John McLaren or among giant redwoods, these routes unveil many sides of the park.

Opposite: ***Heroes Grove was planted in memory of those who died in World War I. Its redwood trees are now more than a century old.***

WALKS & HIKES

1. In the Steps of John McLaren
2. Peace, Love, and Flowers
3. Roses and Redwoods
4. Chasing Waterfalls
5. Medieval Monastery Stone Hunt
6. Coyote Valley
7. Happy Trails and Historic Haunts
8. Chain of Lakes
9. Hidden in Plain Sight: The Northwest Corner
10. The Northern Edge
11. The Southern Edge

If you need a route that sticks to paths that work with a wheelchair, stroller, or mobility device, try **In the Steps of John McLaren** (1.5 miles). It's a classic. If you've got just one day in the park, **Peace, Love, and Flowers** (2 miles) takes you on a less obvious exploration of the eastern end. **Roses and Redwoods** (1 mile) is a shorter and more wooded alternative. You could easily do both in a few hours.

If you're looking for an adventure with kids, the **Medieval Monastery Stone Hunt** (1.3 miles) is for you. Bonus: You can easily add in a visit to the park's premier playground. Need some solitude and nature feels? **Coyote Valley** (2 miles) is a

walk on the wild side of the park, and the **Southern Edge** (4.5 miles) is surprisingly secluded. Want a lot of water? You can't go wrong with the **Chain of Lakes** (2 miles) or **Chasing Waterfalls** (2.5 miles).

If you *think* you know the park like the back of your hand, try **Happy Trails and Historic Haunts** (3 miles) or **Hidden in Plain Sight: The Northwest Corner** (1.5 miles). If it's a clear day and you want as many views of the Golden Gate Bridge as possible, the **Northern Edge** (4 miles) is your best bet. And if you want an epic, all-day exploration of the park, combine the **Northern Edge** *and* **Southern Edge** for an 8.5-mile adventure.

The turn-by-turn directions for these hikes are written with enough detail to be able to follow them alone. However, if something feels unclear, check the map before you get too off track. If needed, go to Google Maps to cross-reference your current location against the map in the book. Find a landmark marked along the route and go from there. The park is only a mile wide, so you can't get too lost!

1 In the Steps of John McLaren

Follow in the footsteps of the park's legendary superintendent on a scenic, stair-free route.	
	START AND END POINT: McLaren Lodge, 501 Stanyan Street
	DISTANCE: 1.3 miles roundtrip
	TIME: 45 minutes
	ACCESSIBILITY: Paved surface, no slopes; appropriate for all ages and abilities
	AMENITIES: Restrooms are in a building next to the Conservatory of Flowers.

SO MUCH OF WHAT we enjoy about the park today is thanks to John McLaren, who shaped and oversaw it for more than half a century as park superintendent. In the long-out-of-print *Golden Gate Park at Your Feet,* author Margot Patterson Doss documented a walk that McLaren did regularly from his home in the park at McLaren Lodge. As you walk in his footsteps and stand eye to eye with a statue of the legend himself, consider what has changed—and what hasn't—in the park since his death in 1943.

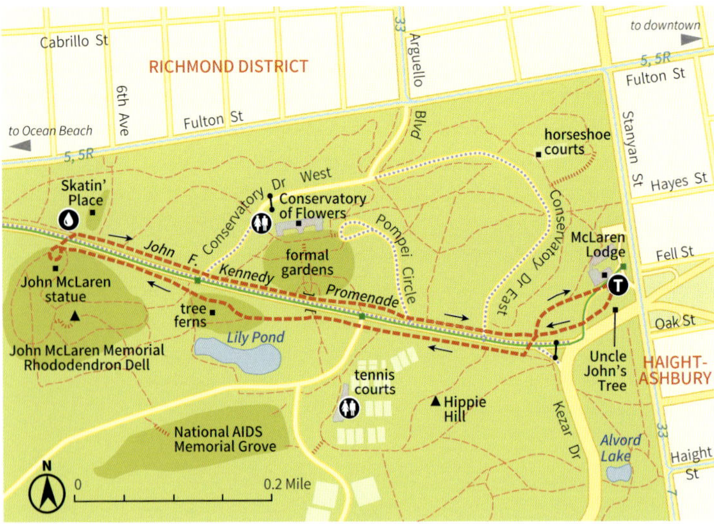

McLaren Lodge

The large stone building in the northeastern corner of the park was built in 1896 to house the park's superintendent and headquarters. John McLaren, who had been made the park superintendent in 1890, got to move right in with his family. He lived there until his death in 1943. Soon after, it was officially renamed McLaren Lodge. When it is open to the public (often on weekdays), step inside and take a peek into the boardroom, with its leather-trimmed walls and giant portrait of McLaren keeping a watchful eye over the decisions being made about the park. McLaren Lodge, along with the Conservatory of Flowers, the Sharon Art Studio, the Powell Street Railway Shelter, and the Bandshell on the Music Concourse, are the park's five Victorian-era buildings still standing.

GETTING THERE

PUBLIC TRANSIT: The 5, 5R, 7, and 33 Muni buses all have stops within a few blocks of McLaren Lodge, with the 33 line offering the closest stop (just one block). The N Judah streetcar has a stop—Carl and Cole—half a mile away. McLaren Lodge is a stop on the Golden Gate Park Shuttle route, so if you're already in the park, this is a good way to get to the lodge (see sfrecpark.org for current hours of service).

BICYCLE: There are bike racks in front of McLaren Lodge. There are also bike-share stations near the lodge at Pompei Circle and JFK Promenade.

DRIVING: There is a curbside drop-off zone in front of McLaren Lodge and an extremely limited amount of free public parking. The closest parking otherwise is street parking on Fulton Street or nearby streets, or the Kezar parking lot on Stanyan Street. There are several free, two-hour ADA spots in front of McLaren Lodge and in a nearby parking zone. On evenings, weekends, and holidays, a limited amount of public parking can be found in the lot behind the lodge.

GET MOVING

This route couldn't be simpler: follow JFK Promenade for about half a mile on the south side of the street, and then return on the north side of the street, with a small detour into the John McLaren Memorial Rhododendron Dell.

Start in front of the steps at **McLaren Lodge** as if you were John McLaren leaving his residence. Take a look up at what's called **Uncle John's Tree**: a Monterey cypress that's almost as old as the park itself. The tree is decorated with lights during the holiday season, a tradition McLaren started as a gift to the children of San Francisco during the Great Depression. (There's a backup tree already growing behind McLaren Lodge.) Turn right, following the path to JFK Promenade, and then

The Wisdom of John McLaren

While I was researching this book, so many things led me back to John McLaren. His fingerprints and footsteps are everywhere in the park. Since McLaren lived to be ninety-six, there's weight to his wisdom, some of which I'll share here.

Don't retire; keep busy. After losing his wife and son, McLaren suffered from depression and failing health. Eventually, he turned to the park for solace and purpose. He oversaw the park for another sixteen years. "Aye keep busy," he often said.

Walk every day. McLaren would take morning walks from his home in the lodge (see p. 160 to do one of his favorites). He spent as much time as possible outside every day, and he never minded picking up a spade and getting dirty.

Plant trees obsessively. "Me boy, if you have nothing to do, go plant a tree and it will grow while you sleep." This was what McLaren's father had told him growing up. And boy, did he take that to heart! "I've planted millions of trees in my time," McLaren told a reporter once at age eighty-seven. "But there are still more to be planted. And I'll plant them

turn right on JFK Promenade. McLaren would have wholeheartedly approved of the removal of private vehicles on this main stretch of road. Throughout his tenure, McLaren fought the encroachment of car traffic in the park, among other things that he felt took away from the feeling of being in nature.

Cross to the sidewalk on the left (south) side of JFK Promenade. Follow the path as it enters the woods and continues into the primordial grove of Tasmanian tree ferns planted by McLaren. This was his favorite part of the park. Continue along the sidewalk until you reach the **John McLaren Memorial Rhododendron Dell**. Walk around the circular path just inside the entrance to the garden. Nestled toward the edge of the adjacent meadow, you'll find a simple statue of McLaren holding a pinecone; it was erected after his death, when the dell was filled with McLaren's favorite flowers. (As mentioned earlier, McLaren didn't like statues in the park and often hid them with plantings, but I'm glad this tribute is here.) Optional: Explore the network of paths deeper in Rhododendron Dell to find some of the quieter areas in the eastern half of the park.

whenever and wherever I can." He is credited with overseeing the planting of more than two million trees in San Francisco during his lifetime.

Talk and listen to kids more than grown-ups. Wealthy people and politicians were always trying to influence McLaren. He preferred talking with children, especially as he got older. McLaren largely judged his success based on how much children enjoyed the park.

Keep things as wild and green as you possibly can. The park may have been a human creation, but even so, McLaren didn't want things to be overly formal or homogenous. He wanted to design the park so people felt like they were truly in nature. Nature "never works in a straight line," said McLaren.

McLaren lived in and oversaw his beloved park until the age of 96. *(Photo courtesy of San Francisco History Center, San Francisco Public Library)*

Cross to the north side of JFK Promenade and take a right to return to the start point. You'll first pass the **Skatin' Place** (more on p. 124). When you reach the large urns that overlook the formal gardens of the **Conservatory of Flowers**, you'll get a similar view to what McLaren saw in his lifetime. The pedestrian tunnel underneath you (now closed) was built in the 1890s. With wonderful acoustics, the entrance on the side farther from the Conservatory is a popular place for musicians to play, especially on Friday afternoons. Continue on JFK Promenade until you return to McLaren Lodge.

2 Peace, Love, and Flowers

Explore Hippie Hill and three stunning dells, which offer many places to sit and enjoy the park's abundant blossoms.	
	START AND END POINT: McLaren Lodge, 501 Stanyan Street
	DISTANCE: 2 miles roundtrip
	TIME: 1 hour minimum
	ACCESSIBILITY: Paved and dirt paths, with some hills and two sets of stairs that can be avoided
	AMENITIES: Restrooms are along the route at the Lisa and Douglas Goldman Tennis Center and in the building next to the Conservatory of Flowers.

JOHN MCLAREN LOVED planting flowers within forest settings. This walk includes Fuchsia Dell (planted toward the end of McLaren's life) and Rhododendron Dell (planted in his honor after his death), both of which showcase McLaren's landscaping style. This walk also gives a nod to the "flower children" (hippies who wore flowers as a symbol of peace and love) of the city by including a destination for many tourists: Hippie Hill. You can even sit under the same tree that Janis Joplin did when she came here to play guitar! When you venture off route where suggested, you'll see just how much of the park's beauty awaits you.

GETTING THERE

PUBLIC TRANSIT: The 5, 5R, 6, 7, and 33 Muni buses all have stops within a few blocks of McLaren Lodge, with the 33 line offering the closest stop (just one block). The N Judah streetcar has a stop—Carl and Cole—half a mile away. McLaren Lodge is a stop on the Golden Gate Park Shuttle route, so if you're already

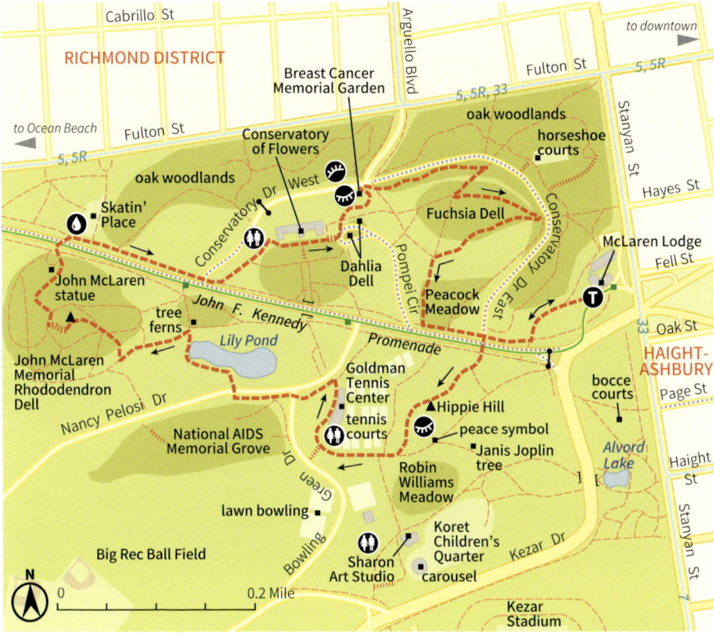

in the park, this is a good way to get to the lodge (see sfrecpark.org for current hours of service).

BICYCLE: There are bike racks in front of McLaren Lodge. There are also bikeshare stations near McLaren Lodge at Pompei Circle and JFK Promenade.

DRIVING: There is a curbside drop-off zone in front of McLaren Lodge and an extremely limited amount of free public parking. The closest parking otherwise is street parking on Fulton Street or nearby streets, or the Kezar parking lot on Stanyan Street. There are several free, two-hour ADA spots in front of McLaren Lodge and in a nearby parking zone. On evenings, weekends, and holidays, a limited amount of public parking can be found in the lot behind the Lodge.

GET MOVING

Start at **McLaren Lodge** facing the street. Take the path to the far right and walk to JFK Promenade. Cross to the far side of JFK Promenade, turn right onto the sidewalk, and immediately take the paved path that leads away from the street. Continue up the path, going right at the Y intersection. Shortly, you will arrive at the top of **Hippie Hill**.

Hippie Hill became a hangout during 1967's Summer of Love thanks to the nearby Haight-Ashbury neighborhood, which was the epicenter of the counterculture movement. The hill was a place for music and self-expression, and it still has a free-spirited feel today. If you're there on a nice weekend afternoon, there will likely be a drum circle at the base of the hill near a large peace symbol painted on the sidewalk; drummers have been a mainstay here for decades. The shaggy elm tree, the only tree along the path leading away from the base of Hippie Hill, is said to be where rock icon Janis Joplin sat and played guitar in the 1960s.

At the top of Hippie Hill, pause and look around you. To your left is a view of **Robin Williams Meadow**, named in honor of the comedian (1951–2014) who got his start in San Francisco and performed at the park's first Comedy Day. The **Sharon Art Studio** and **Koret Children's Quarter** are across Robin Williams Meadow.

You'll find drummers and dancers on most warm, sunny days at the bottom of Hippie Hill; just follow your ears.

Stand eye-to-eye with the legendary John McLaren on this walk in his footsteps.

Continue down Hippie Hill, curving to the left as the path descends. At the bottom of the hill, take the first path to the right and follow it as it curves around the courts and to the front of the **Goldman Tennis Center** (more on p. 122); pop inside if you need a restroom—these are really nice ones. The Goldman Tennis Center was completely rebuilt in 2021, but there have been courts here since 1894.

Continue until you pass through three silver gateposts as the path reaches the street. Then immediately turn left on the sidewalk along Nancy Pelosi Drive. You will pass over a long-closed, historical pedestrian tunnel. Continue a short distance to reach the intersection of Bowling Green Drive and Nancy Pelosi Drive at 0.5 mile.

Take the crosswalk toward the **De Laveaga Dell / AIDS Memorial Grove** sign (see p. 86 for more), but don't head into the grove; instead, continue on the sidewalk running along Nancy Pelosi Drive. You will soon see a tall green sign across the street marking the entrance to Lily Pond and Fern Dell. Cross the road to reach the sign. Follow the path beneath the sign down toward **Lily Pond**.

Downhill, you will come to Lily Pond, which was created from a quarry dug for stones to pave park paths in the early years. After passing along the pond, turn left and follow the paved path up to the top of the hill, then turn right downhill to enter the **John McLaren Memorial Rhododendron Dell**, where hundreds of kinds of McLaren's favorite flower fill twenty acres of forested hills. Continue straight until you reach a long, paved uphill ramp on your left (at 0.8 mile). Follow the ramp to the top of the hill to look out over the dell, and don't miss the wisdom about aging inscribed on one of the benches.

Go down the hill on the stairs opposite the ramp you came up on. At the bottom, turn right, and then go left at the first intersection to wind your way out of the

Rhododendron Dell. As you head out, look for the **statue of John McLaren** set back toward the woods on your left. Note that the low wall behind the statue is made of monastery stones (more on p. 180).

When the paved path reaches **JFK Promenade**, cross it. Turn right and stroll along the sidewalk on the left (north) side of JFK Promenade until you reach the intersection with Conservatory Drive West. Cross Conservatory Drive West, then take the first paved path to your left. It will lead you toward the **Conservatory of Flowers** (on your way, there are restrooms in the small building to the left of the Conservatory).

Continue past the Conservatory entrance on your left and take the stairs down to the **Dahlia Dell** (more on p. 84). You will be going up the stairs immediately to your left. But first, just for fun, look for the stone shaped like California in the stone wall at the base of the hillside dahlia garden.

Now go up the aforementioned stairs and follow the paved path up the hill to Conservatory Drive (on your left will be the **Breast Cancer Memorial Garden**). Turn right on Conservatory Drive and go down the paved path. About 50 feet down on your left, you'll see the small sign to the unpaved **Oak Woodlands Trail** (more on p. 148). Take this path until it intersects with the road, then take a sharp right (at 1.5 miles), going downhill on the next paved path. Turn left on the paved trail at the bottom of the hill. The trail passes through the center of the expansive **Fuchsia Dell**, with fuchsia plantings on both sides of the trail. San Francisco's cool and foggy summers create the ideal environment for these beautiful flowers, which bloom from May to November.

Just before the trail reaches the road, take the sharp right on the trail that heads upward on a small ridge, with the Fuchsia Dell downhill on your right. When the trail nears the bottom of the hill, turn left at the Y intersection with **Peacock Meadow** on your left. When the path ends at JFK Promenade, turn left to return to **McLaren Lodge** along JFK Promenade.

Off the main paved trail of Fuchsia Dell, you'll find dozens of types of fuchsia along inviting paths through towering redwood trees.

3 Roses and Redwoods

Stop and smell the roses before exploring two redwood groves, plus a secret pond and some locals-only trails.	
	START AND END POINT: Entrance to the Rose Garden on JFK Promenade at Funston Avenue
	DISTANCE: 1 mile roundtrip
	TIME: 1 hour
	ACCESSIBILITY: Mostly on dirt and wood-chip paths, with some small changes in elevation
	AMENITIES: Restrooms are near the Rose Garden in a small building at 14th Avenue East picnic area.

YOU DON'T HAVE to drive over the Golden Gate Bridge to Muir Woods to experience the California coastal redwoods. The park has several groves, including two century-old memorial ones on either side of the Rose Garden: Heroes Grove and the lesser-known Redwood Memorial Grove. This short walk brings flowers and the forest together.

GETTING THERE

PUBLIC TRANSIT: The closest bus lines are the 5, 5R, 28, and 28R, which all have stops at Park Presidio Boulevard and Fulton Street, just a couple minutes' walk from the start. The 31 and 44 Muni buses have stops less than a ten-minute walk from the Rose Garden. The free Golden Gate Park Shuttle directly serves the Rose Garden with a stop directly in front of it.

BICYCLE: There are bike racks just west of the Rose Garden by the 14th Avenue East Meadow on JFK Promenade.

DRIVING: There is a curbside drop-off zone by the bus shelter on the park side of Fulton Street at Park Presidio Boulevard. There are also red drop-off zones abutting the Rose Garden on Fulton Street between Park Presidio Boulevard and Funston Avenue. You can park at the Music Concourse parking garage, and there's some street parking on Blue Heron Lake Drive and along Fulton Street. There are two ADA parking spots by the Rose Garden on the park side of Fulton Street at Park Presidio Boulevard. A more reliable option for ADA parking is the free ADA lot in the Music Concourse or the paid ADA lot in the Music Concourse garage, with direct service via the Golden Gate Park Shuttle to the Rose Garden.

Oriented to maximize sun and minimize wind, the Rose Garden is in bloom May through June, with additional blossoms appearing in September and December.

GET MOVING

Start at the **Rose Garden** sign along JFK Promenade. Facing the Rose Garden, to your right is the dense **Heroes Grove** redwood forest. On Memorial Day in 1919, more than 10,000 people gathered to plant these trees to remember the San Francisco sons and daughters who died in World War I. John McLaren planted the first tree at the ceremony. Optional: Wander around this peaceful grove of century-old trees and find the simple stone memorial nestled in among them.

Take the paved path from **JFK Promenade** into the Rose Garden, which was planted in 1961 on what was previously a road for cars heading into the park. In the middle of the Rose Garden is a large circular flower bed, carefully tended with other types of flowers so there's always something blooming, even when it's not rose season (roses peak here from mid-May to July, plus in September, with some varieties blooming in December). As you face the circle, you'll see a fence along the edge of the garden with two doorways. Go to the left doorway (the doorposts are labeled "James Galway" and "Grandmother's Hat" roses) and walk through it and the opening in the hedge behind it to a meadow. Turn left and take the wood-chip path up a slope, with the gardener's shed on your left.

Entering the woods, you'll see a tiny pond in a small grove on the left. If you visited Golden Gate Park prior to 2024, you wouldn't have seen it. Created by gardeners in the hole left when a large tree fell over and uprooted, it has been landscaped into a hidden gem that's barely visible from the road. Continue down the path past the pond, walk straight across JFK Promenade, and take the paved path leading up the small hill away from the road. As you reach the top of the slope, take the wide wood-chip path on the right.

Follow this path as it wanders through the trees, with the **Pioneer East Meadow** on your right. It's a popular place for picnics and weddings. Eventually, you'll see the back side of the **Pioneer Log Cabin** (more on p. 177). Follow the path as it continues slightly uphill. At the paved path, turn left.

When you reach Blue Heron Lake Drive, take the crosswalk across the street to continue on the sidewalk straight ahead. You'll see the Blue Heron Boat House on your left and restrooms on the right. Cross the parking lot and find the paved path on your right just past the restrooms. Follow the path to JFK Promenade. Walk

across the road and go straight to take the old paved service road ahead of you. Follow the road until it ends, then turn right at the T.

Continue along the trail. Despite Highway 1 being just a few feet over the wall on your left, the majesty of the trees on the right and the dense vegetation help give the feeling of being far from the rush of traffic. **Redwood Memorial Grove** is a few steps off the trail to your right. Step in, look up, and feel the serenity of the living memorial planted in 1927 to honor locals who died in World War I; more names were added after World War II.

Back on the trail, you'll see **Doughboy Meadow's** statue and flagpole to your right through the trees. When you see a dirt path coming through a wide opening in the hedges on your right at 0.7 mile (the cars on the highway will have just become visible through a gap on your left), turn and follow the path across a little meadow, and then turn right on the first paved path.

When you reach the sidewalk along JFK Promenade, make a sharp left back onto a dirt path up along a ridge. Eventually, you'll reach a fork; follow the path to the right to go sharply down a slope to the paved path, turn right, and then take the next right back into the **Rose Garden** to where you started.

The Pioneer Log Cabin was built using redwood trees from far Northern California. *(Photo by Jim Watkins)*

Hike the paths right next to Huntington Falls for unique views on your way to the highest point in the park: the top of Strawberry Hill. *(Photo by Jim Watkins)*

4 Chasing Waterfalls

Trace a path between the park's two biggest waterfalls with a stop at the picturesque falls of Lloyd Lake.

START AND END POINT: Entrance to the Rose Garden on JFK Promenade at Funston Avenue

DISTANCE: 2.5 miles roundtrip

TIME: 1.5 hours

ACCESSIBILITY: One set of stairs, but otherwise a mostly flat walk on paved and dirt paths

AMENITIES: Restrooms can be found near the start in the 14th Avenue East Meadow at JFK Promenade. Restrooms and concessions are available at Blue Heron Lake Boat House.

THE TWO MAJOR WATERFALLS on this hike are worthy destinations—no explanation needed. But the story of Huntington Falls connects Golden Gate park: the top of

Strawberry Hill. directly to America's national parks, as longtime park superintendent John McLaren happened to be friends with conservationist John Muir. Muir had championed the creation of Yosemite National Park in 1890. On a hike with Muir in California's Sierra Nevada around that time, McLaren is said to have been inspired by all the cascading waters. He returned to San Francisco on a mission to bring one to the park.

McLaren oversaw (and raised the money for) the construction of Huntington Falls, plus the lake, island, and bridges around the existing Strawberry Hill in time for the 1894 California Midwinter International Exposition. The 100-foot-tall Huntington Falls still impresses visitors today, as do the fifty-foot-plus Rainbow Falls and other water features you'll see on this hike.

GETTING THERE

PUBLIC TRANSIT: The closest bus lines are the 5, 5R, 28, and 28R, which all have stops at Park Presidio Boulevard and Fulton Street, just a couple minutes' walk from the start. The 31 and 44 Muni buses have stops less than a ten-minute walk from the Rose Garden. The free Golden Gate Park Shuttle serves the Rose Garden with a stop directly in front of it.

BICYCLE: There are bike racks just west of the Rose Garden by the 14th Avenue East Meadow on JFK Promenade.

DRIVING: There is a curbside drop-off zone by the bus shelter on the park side of Fulton Street at Park Presidio Boulevard. There are also red drop-off zones abutting the Rose Garden on Fulton Street between Park Presidio Boulevard and Funston Avenue. You can park at the Music Concourse parking garage, and there's some street parking on Blue Heron Lake Drive and along Fulton Street. There are two ADA parking spots by the Rose Garden on the park side of Fulton Street at Park Presidio Boulevard. A more reliable option for ADA parking is the free ADA lot in the Music Concourse or the paid ADA lot in the Music Concourse garage, with direct service via the Golden Gate Park Shuttle to the Rose Garden.

GET MOVING

Start at the **Rose Garden** entrance on JFK Promenade. Facing away from the roses, cross JFK Promenade. Turn right on the sidewalk, then turn left on the next paved path going uphill. Turn

All the Waterfalls

Who doesn't love a good water feature? Here's your checklist if you want to hit them all.

THE BIG FALLS:

- ☐ Huntington Falls at Blue Heron Lake
- ☐ Rainbow Falls on JFK Promenade near Crossover Drive
- ☐ The 800-foot cascading creek at Middle Lake

THE SMALLER FALLS:

- ☐ Multiple spots in the Japanese Tea Garden
- ☐ At the far western end of the National AIDS Memorial Grove
- ☐ At Lloyd Lake
- ☐ At Metson Lake
- ☐ Next to the Zellerbach Garden of Perennials in the Botanical Garden

WALKS AND HIKES WITH AT LEAST ONE WATERFALL:

- ☐ Coyote Valley
- ☐ Happy Trails and Historic Haunts
- ☐ Chain of Lakes

right on the first paved path and go up the stairs. At the top of the stairs, the path forks—take the path to the left and you will almost immediately reach **Blue Heron Lake Drive East**. Cross the road on the crosswalk and turn left on the sidewalk along the lake's edge.

You'll see the tall trees of **Strawberry Hill** rising from the middle of the lake, and the postcard-worthy **Huntington Falls** will come into view across Blue Heron Lake. From a distance, the waterfall looks so natural that many people are shocked to find it is completely artificial, powered by pumps and fed by a reservoir at the top of the hill.

Keep walking along the lake's edge. After about a quarter mile, the lake will narrow. Coming up on your right will be the unmistakable **Rustic Bridge**, built of red chert rocks mined from the park. Turn right to cross the bridge (at 0.5 mile), then turn right again when you reach the island. Continue until you reach the **Chinese Pavilion**. It was donated by San Francisco's sister city Taipei in 1976. As a bonus, there's a small waterfall in the pool surrounding the pavilion. Continue on the path, crossing the stones directly in front of **Huntington Falls**.

Find a bonus small waterfall in the pool surrounding the colorful Chinese Pavilion. *(Photo by Robert Ho)*

Optional: Go up the stairs immediately to the right side of the waterfall and hike up to more overlooks and additional cascades. At the very top, hummingbirds are often spotted bathing in the waterfall. Continue to the reservoir at the top of the falls, and then follow the path to the top of Strawberry Hill. From different vantages here, you'll find views of downtown, the Golden Gate Bridge, Sutro Tower, and the ocean. Return via the same stairs.

Continue on the path along the edge of the island until you reach the simple **Roman Bridge**. Cross the bridge, then turn immediately left to follow the lakeshore. Soon you'll see clusters of rental boats from the **Blue Heron Boat House**. Follow the path toward it, then turn right just before the boat house to reach the parking lot below, at 1 mile. (Restrooms are on the opposite side of the parking lot, but if you go, return to the side of the street closest to Blue Heron Lake).

With the restrooms on your left, follow the sidewalk along the right side of the parking lot. The sidewalk will end at a crosswalk directing you to a paved path into the woods. Follow this path as it continues through a shady grove with stone walls on either side. The path curves to the left. Soon on your right you will see the **Pioneer Log Cabin**, built in 1911 by the Association of Pioneer Women of California (since disbanded). The cabin, which is made with redwood trees, was designed by the Reid brothers. These architects also designed the Bandshell on the Music Concourse and the Fairmont Union Square Hotel. The cabin has been used for various purposes over the years and is not currently open to the public.

When you reach JFK Promenade, cross to the other side. Before you turn left to follow the sidewalk, notice the ornamental plants, including many succulents, planted along the bushes here. Optional: Find paths nearby that lead behind the garden to explore this special place before continuing. This book is (un)officially naming it **Marta's Garden** in recognition of the lead volunteer who created and maintains it (and who happens to share my name).

Continue along the sidewalk. Soon you will arrive at **Rainbow Falls**, which at the time of publication has an exquisite metal sculpture of a sea serpent named Naga below it. Built in 1930, the falls were originally lit with colored lights, hence the name. The lights didn't last, but the name did (note that the water is green due to algae, not dye). Look up to the top of Rainbow Falls; you'll get a glimpse of the Celtic **Prayer Book Cross**, another item installed for the 1894 California Midwinter International Exposition. Follow the stream downhill from Rainbow Falls, going under the bridge and then crossing Transverse Drive. Staying on the sidewalk, look for the **Mystery Spot** of Golden Gate Park: just as the stream ahead of you starts to curve, it will appear as if it is flowing uphill!

Continue walking along the stream until it becomes a waterfall into **Lloyd Lake**, which was created in 1905. Turn right to cross the stream on the stones and circle the entire lake. You'll pass the famous **Portals of the Past**; this was the grand entrance of a Nob Hill mansion destroyed in the 1906 earthquake, installed in the park in 1909 to remember this defining and devastating event for San Francisco.

Walk east on JFK Promenade back to your start point at the Rose Garden. Note: You can also take the Golden Gate Park Shuttle back from the intersection of JFK Promenade and Transverse Drive to the Rose Garden, which would shorten this hike to 1.3 miles total.

5 Medieval Monastery Stone Hunt

This search for ancient monastery stones scattered throughout the park will bring you to surprising and secluded areas.

START AND END POINT: The entrance of the San Francisco County Fair Building at 1199 9th Avenue

DISTANCE: 1.3 miles roundtrip

TIME: 1 hour

ACCESSIBILITY: Includes unpaved and uneven surfaces, including narrow trails; not recommended for strollers or wheelchairs

AMENITIES: Public restrooms are available in Big Rec Ball Field and inside the paid area of the Botanical Garden.

THE HISTORY OF the ancient carved stones found throughout Golden Gate Park is fascinating (see "The Story Behind the Stones" sidebar, below). These slices of history are also fun to search for, and this walk passes dozens of monastery stones. You'll climb along a burbling creek through coastal redwoods and visit a quiet forest of oak woodlands that few people ever make it to—all within a stone's throw of the park's more popular eastern attractions.

GETTING THERE

PUBLIC TRANSIT: The 7 and 44 Muni buses have stops less than one block away at 9th and Lincoln. The N Judah streetcar stops about two blocks away at Irving

Street and 9th Avenue, and the 6 and the 43 Muni buses both have stops less than a ten-minute walk away.

BICYCLE: Abundant bike racks are in front of the County Fair Building by the Botanical Garden, and a small number of racks are to the right of the Main Gate of the Botanical Garden.

DRIVING: There's a passenger drop-off and pick-up zone in front of the County Fair Building. You can park on MLK Drive, on Nancy Pelosi Drive, and at the nearby Music Concourse parking garage. On weekends, this is a very congested area of the park to drive to or through.

Shakespeare Garden

Despite being so close to the Music Concourse, the Shakespeare Garden is easily missed; it's just to the west of the California Academy of Sciences. This charming garden—maybe the park's most romantic—dates back to 1928. And if you appreciate flowers, literature, or the theatre, you should step inside. At the far end, you can stand face to face with a bust of William Shakespeare and read a wall covered in the Bard's most enduring quotes. The garden is also full of flowers and plants from Shakespeare's sonnets and plays: poppies, pansies, primroses, violets, and many more. This garden was brought to life by trailblazing botanist (and friend of John McLaren) Alice Eastwood. Inside the garden, you'll find a bench dedicated to her.

(Photo by Robert Ho)

GET MOVING

In the middle of the plaza in front of the **County Fair Building**, you will find a low garden with a variety of monastery stones scattered in it. This is a great opportunity to familiarize yourself with what the gray, hand-carved pieces of limestone generally look like.

Now walk toward the Main Gate of the **Botanical Garden**. Take the crosswalk directly in front of the Main Gate to the other side of MLK Drive. Turn immediately left and continue on the sidewalk until you cross the next intersection at Nancy Pelosi Drive. After crossing, continue a short distance along the sidewalk and then take the first paved path to the right. Soon you will see the **Shakespeare Garden** on your right and a bench surrounded by monastery stones on your left. Optional: Walk into the charming and romantic Shakespeare Garden.

Continue on the path, and after passing the Shakespeare Garden, take the next right. The California Academy of Sciences will be on your left. When you reach Nancy

The Story Behind the Stones

The fascinating reason the monastery stones are in Golden Gate Park goes all the way back to 1167, when the Santa María de Óvila monastery was founded by King Alfonso VIII of Castile in Spain. It was a complex of intricately designed buildings made by monks out of carved stone, including a cathedral. That's why it caught the eye of William Randolph Hearst's art dealer in the 1920s. Although the monastery was empty and had fallen into disrepair, it was gorgeous.

Wealthy businessman Hearst had already built one castle in California, but wanted another even more spectacular one in Northern California. So Hearst purchased the Santa María de Óvila monastery. He had it dismantled, and then eleven ships carried the carefully labeled stones all the way to San Francisco. But Hearst's plan to rebuild and repurpose the ancient Santa María de Óvila monastery stones was not to be. The Great Depression ended Hearst's empire, and he ran out of money before architects could even finish a design. Eventually, he gifted the stones to the City of San Francisco. And thus the connection to Golden Gate Park began to take shape.

A new idea emerged in the early 1940s: why not rebuild the monastery in Golden Gate Park and make it a museum of medieval art? Somewhat controversial plans moved forward, and the crates of stones were moved into Golden Gate Park. But a series of suspicious fires in

Pelosi Drive, turn left immediately onto the wood-chip path into the Academy's native plant garden with benches carved into logs. Optional: Explore this garden by walking around the exterior of the building.

After the wood-chip path returns to the sidewalk, take the midblock crosswalk across Nancy Pelosi Drive. Turn immediately left on the sidewalk and continue along Nancy Pelosi Drive. With the road on your left, keep an eye out for a large group of monastery stones edging a garden between the sidewalk and the road. When you

The Botanical Garden is full of monastery stones; the Rhododendron Garden has a pavilion made from them, designed by Edwin Hamilton. *(Photo by Jim Watkins)*

the 1940s and 1950s ultimately made putting most of the monastery buildings back together impossible. However, the cathedral's portal was successfully reassembled in 1965 and became part of an entrance to the de Young Museum in Golden Gate Park.

When the original de Young Museum was demolished in 2002, the portal was donated to the University of San Francisco. (You can see it at the school's nearby campus.) In 2013, the chapter house was successfully rebuilt at the Abbey of New Clairvaux in Vina, California, using two-thirds of the original stones. Somewhere in the midst of all that, the monastery stones were used for landscaping in Golden Gate Park. You can find many of them in and around the Japanese Tea Garden and the Botanical Garden, but keep an eye out everywhere!

to Stanyan St
Lily Pond
main entrance
Bowling Green Dr
to downtown
National AIDS Memorial Grove
circular dirt area
nursery
circular stone plaza
Nancy Pelosi Dr
circle with chime
handball courts
Big Rec Ball Field
Martin Luther King, Jr. Dr
3rd Ave
5th Ave
Hugo St
Lincoln Way
7th Ave
8th Ave
9th Ave
44
native plant garden
California Academy of Sciences
shed
Shakespeare Garden
one-way
Music Concourse Dr
Main Gate
library
County Fair Building
SUNSET DISTRICT
Garden of Fragrance
Great Meadow
Temperate Asia
Music Concourse
Hagiwara Tea Garden Dr
deYoung Museum
Ancient Plant Garden
Rhododendron Garden
12th Ave
7, 29
JAPANESE TEA GARDEN
North Gate
Australia
SAN FRANCISCO BOTANICAL GARDEN
California Native Garden
0.2 Mile
0
John F. Kennedy Promenade
Martin Luther King, Jr. Dr
Andean Cloud Forest
Conifer Lawn
Nursery
Lincoln Way
Blue Heron Lake Dr
SE Asian Cloud Forest
Redwood Grove
to Ocean Beach
Succulent Garden
Blue Heron Lake
Children's Garden
N
to Ocean Beach
MONASTERY STONES
Large area
Small area

reach the intersection with Bowling Green Drive at about 0.8 mile, you'll see the main entrance to the **National AIDS Memorial Grove** immediately on your right (see p. 86). Take a sharp right to enter the grove on the main path straight down—not the paved, wheelchair-accessible path.

As you head down the path, take the first trail that goes off to your right, which is lined with a long chain of thin monastery stones. At the end of the path, take a big step up to a seating area, then take the stone stairs back down to the main path. (Note: The stair risers are *not* monastery stones but rather repurposed granite street curbs; you'll see remnants of red paint). Turn right on the main path to continue through the grove's long valley.

At the far end of the valley, you'll find yourself standing in a large, circular dirt area. Straight ahead you'll see a creekbed with paths and coastal redwoods on either side heading uphill. Take the path uphill on the right side of the creek, and hike to the top of the creek.

At the end of the trail, as you are about to step into the circular stone plaza, look around your feet for monastery stones, which may be hidden under leaves. From this circle, take the stairs up on the left. You will reach yet another circular stone plaza, where you'll see an 8-foot-tall pole—that's a remembrance chime. Exit the circle to the left, then take an immediate right onto the dirt path.

Continue straight (slightly downhill) into the oak woodlands, keeping an eye out for scattered monastery stones along the trail. After a short walk, you will come upon a monastery stone hotspot! A circle of stones marks a sacred space for the Druid community; this is also where Monarch the grizzly bear once lived (more on p. 146). Optional: Explore the surrounding woods, and you'll find many more monastery stones scattered around.

Head downhill through the circle of stones, exiting by the gray-and-green concrete **handball courts** building at 1 mile. Reaching the outdoor paved court, look to your left to see a row of monastery stones along the edge of the court. Follow this edge and walk clockwise (right) around the building. You will see a shed and a larger restroom building to your left. Walk between the large trees toward the restroom. The long stone wall between the two buildings is made of monastery stones.

Walk between the two buildings and then follow the path to the right around the outside edge of **Big Rec Ball Field**. As the path approaches the street, you will see the entrance to the Botanical Garden across MLK Drive. Turn right on the dirt path. Immediately take the crosswalk to the Main Gate of the Botanical Garden.

You're now a stone's throw (pun intended) from your starting place in front of the County Fair Building and at the end of this walk. However, for your grand finale of stone-searching, you can step just past the Main Gate and find many monastery stones in the gardens and paths *before* going through the admission area.

Optional: If you're really into finding monastery stones, the Botanical Garden has more of them than any other place in the park. Once inside the Botanical Garden, the three stoniest spots are the pavilion with low stone walls and a fountain immediately to the left after going through the ticket gate near the Main Gate; the spectacular pavilion in the Rhododendron Garden; and the stone walls and stairs in the Succulent Garden (see the map on p. 182).

6 Coyote Valley

Explore the wildest section of the park for solitude, scenic lakes, and dense forests.

START AND END POINT: The Breon Gate entrance of Golden Gate Park at 19th Avenue and Lincoln Way

DISTANCE: 2 miles roundtrip

TIME: 1 hour minimum

ACCESSIBILITY: Mostly on dirt paths, with a few rough and steep sections

AMENITIES: Restrooms are by the southern entrance to the Polo Field, a short detour from Metson Lake.

THE WESTERN HALF of the park is the wilder side. And Coyote Valley—the area between Mallard, Metson, and Elk Glen Lakes—is the wildest part. This walk roughly follows the edge of the region, but you may be inspired to explore the unmarked paths in the area. You'll feel far from the city on these trails, and you're more likely to see wildlife than people in many spots.

GETTING THERE

PUBLIC TRANSIT: The 7, 28, 28R, and 29 Muni buses have stops at 19th Ave. and Lincoln Way. The N streetcar stops two blocks away. It is less than a ten-minute walk from the Golden Gate Park shuttle stop at Transverse Drive.

BICYCLE: Bike racks are at the Mothers' Meadow restrooms on MLK Drive east of Transverse Drive.

DRIVING: Street parking can be found along MLK Drive west of Transverse Drive.

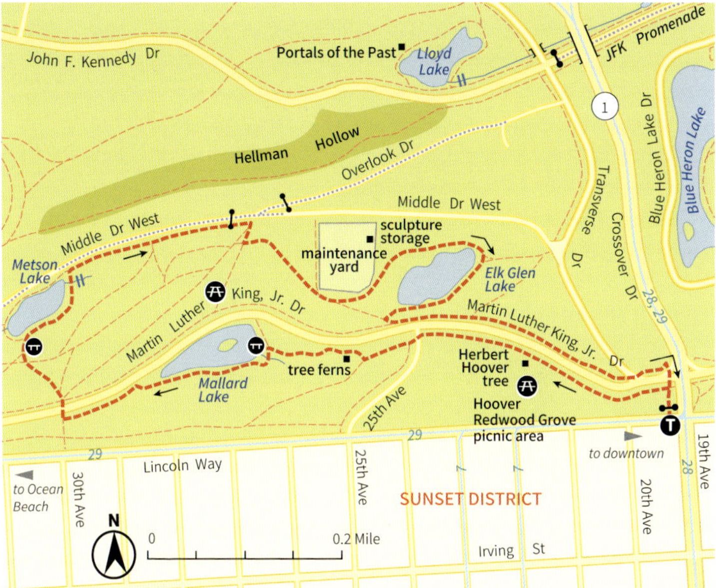

GET MOVING

Facing the park's entrance at 19th Avenue, enter the park on the left side of the intersection through the tunnel in the stone gate. Turn left on MLK Drive and follow the sidewalk as it winds away and then back toward the street. You'll pass the grassy Hoover Redwood Grove picnic area on your left. Look for the Herbert Hoover tree near the sidewalk—an impressive coastal redwood tree planted in 1935 to honor the former president's work protecting California's ancient redwoods.

Continue as the sidewalk changes from asphalt to gravel. At the next intersection, you will cross 25th Avenue (unsigned) and walk straight to continue uphill on the dirt path. Take the very first path on your right to go downhill into a dell of tree ferns and *Gunnera* plants, with their giant, sandpapery leaves. Veer right at the fork, keeping the road on your right. The path will begin to go downhill, and soon **Mallard Lake** will come into view. This is the only natural lake that still exists in the park.

Approaching Mallard Lake, just before the viewing bench, turn left on the path and cross the little stream on the stepping stones. Continue around the left side of the lake. Follow the lovely, shaded path until you return to MLK Drive. At MLK

Drive, the trail ends; turn left to walk on the grass along the left side of the road, as there's no sidewalk here. At the next crosswalk, cross to the other side of MLK Drive and take the gravel path ahead of you. You'll see two forks in the path ahead; veer left at both of them. Continue uphill on this path, cross the wide dirt road, and continue straight uphill toward the green benches that indicate the edge of **Metson Lake**, which was John McLaren's favorite lake.

Metson Lake was built as a reservoir in 1908 to store water pumped by the Murphy Windmill (the southern windmill across from Ocean Beach) to irrigate the park. At the benches, turn right to follow the path along the lake. Despite its artificial nature, it creates important habitat along the water's edge for California native riparian and wetland plantings. Continue on the trail beside the lake; you'll cross an artificial stream just before the path ends (at 0.8 mile). Turn right on Middle Drive West.

Walk along the car-free Middle Drive West. After passing through the yellow gateposts and just before the road forks, take the next paved path on your right at 1.1 mile. Almost immediately, you will see two narrow footpaths going downhill. Take the second path (it's less steep). Walk down and then up the valley. When

Metson Lake was John McLaren's favorite of the park's ten lakes, and it's mine, too. *(Photo by Jim Watkins)*

you reach the chain-link fence around a park maintenance yard, stay right to keep the fence on your left, then turn left at the next fork. Through the fence, you'll see there's a storage yard, and you might even spy some old sculptures from bygone eras in the park.

As the path leads downhill, you'll soon see **Elk Glen Lake** on your right, named for the elk that used to live here to add to the park's Wild West feel (they were moved to the newly built San Francisco Zoo around 1930, joining some zebras, monkeys, and elephants that had also previously lived in the park).

Walk clockwise around the lake, staying close to the water. After the small, sandy beach, continue straight until the path ends at the gravel road. Turn left to return to MLK Drive. Turn left on MLK Drive and stay on the northern sidewalk to return to the start point.

7 Happy Trails and Historic Haunts

Journey through time on these bridle paths to some of the park's most enduring activities and historic happenings.

START AND END POINT: Park entrance at 22nd Avenue and Fulton Street

DISTANCE: 3 miles roundtrip

TIME: 1.5 to 2 hours

ACCESSIBILITY: Mostly wide unpaved roads, with some hills

AMENITIES: Restrooms are at both the Polo Field and the Anglers Lodge.

THE POLO FIELD and the land around it host many of the park's lesser-known activities, from disc golf to fly casting, along with pastoral paths once traveled by horses and buggies. This hike is a mix of scenic solitude and surprising stops—plus you are almost guaranteed to spot horses outside the police stables.

GETTING THERE

PUBLIC TRANSIT: The 5 and 5R Muni buses stop right at the route's start point at 22nd and Fulton. The 29 and 31 Muni buses stop within a few blocks, and the Golden Gate Park Shuttle's stop at Transverse is a five-minute walk.

BICYCLE: There's a sidewalk bike rack across the street from the start point.

DRIVING: Street parking is available on JFK Drive west of Transverse Drive.

RICHMOND DISTRICT
SUNSET DISTRICT
22nd Ave
25th Ave
30th Ave
36th Ave
23rd Ave
34th Ave
41st Ave
Cabrillo St
Fulton St
Irving St
Lincoln Way
Sunset Blvd
to downtown
to Ocean Beach
Crossover Dr
Transverse Dr
Overlook Dr
Middle Dr West
Martin Luther King, Jr. Dr
John F. Kennedy Dr
Chain of Lakes Dr East
Middle Dr East
Lloyd Lake
Portals of the Past
Elk Glen Lake
Mallard Lake
Metson Lake
Spreckels Lake
Middle Lake
South Lake
disc golf course
Marx Meadow
Hellman Hollow
Lindley Meadow
Polo Field
velodrome track
multiuse trail
police horse stables
Anglers Lodge
casting pools
bison paddock
Cascade Trail
Lake Loop Trail
First Parcourse station
Parcourse stations
0
0.2 Mile
N
1
5R
29
7
8
12

GET MOVING

Start the walk at the 22nd Avenue and Fulton Street entrance to the park by the bus shelter. Optional: If it's a clear day, take a moment to walk to the far side of 22nd Avenue and look north for a view of both towers of the Golden Gate Bridge.

Take the wide path into the park and across Crossover Drive and Transverse Drive. Continue into the woods ahead of you on the wide dirt path. This was originally created as a bridle path for horseback riding. Lloyd Lake will become visible on your left below the trail. Soon you'll find yourself walking through the **disc golf course** (watch for flying discs at all times of day). Look down to **Lloyd Lake** on the left to see the backside of the **Portals of the Past** columns (which you'll see on the **Chasing Waterfalls** hike)—all that remained of a grand San Francisco home after the 1906 earthquake. The columns were placed here in remembrance of the city's defining disaster.

Continue all the way down the hill, staying on the wide path. Cross the paved JFK Drive and continue on the trail as it goes uphill. Below you on your left is **Hellman Hollow**, named for Warren Hellman, the patron of the annual, free Hardly

The Polo Field was built largely in the early 1900s for bicycle racing; it still serves as a velodrome today.

Strictly Bluegrass festival (more on p. 102). Soon you'll enter the still-maintained parcourse exercise route, built in 1980 (this outdoor fitness trend started in San Francisco in the 1970s and became popular again during the pandemic).

To the right of the parcourse rings station (#8) at 0.5 mile, there's a picnic area made of logs at the top of the hill with nice views. Turn right at the next fork, continuing along the parcourse route. Passing the parcourse vault bar (#12) on the right, continue straight on the wide dirt path. Through the trees on your left is the

The Polo Field (Golden Gate Park Stadium)

The impetus for building the Polo Field actually wasn't polo, but rather to host harness horse and bicycle racing. Construction began in 1903 and meant the removal of 150,000 cubic yards of sand! But the great earthquake on April 18, 1906, halted the project, with nearby Speedway Meadow (now Hellman Hollow) becoming one of the park's refugee camps for those who had lost their homes.

Work soon got back on track as a way to show that the city would rise from the ashes. On July 4, 1906, approximately 20,000 people came to the grand opening of what was named Golden Gate Park Stadium. They celebrated again one year later with 100,000 people. Big moments and big crowds continued over the years. On September 11, 1911, more than 10,000 people gathered here to see the first west-to-east transcontinental airplane flight take off (it was an unsuccessful attempt, though the pilot lived).

The Polo Field was the epicenter of the West Coast's bicycle racing scene, especially from the 1930s to 1950s. (A fun aside: the bicycles in these races had no brakes or gears, and the front wheel didn't turn!) The 1930s was also when polo actually began to be played in the stadium and people started to call it Polo Field. The name stuck, despite polo fading out by the 1970s.

In 1967, tens of thousands of people went to the Polo Field for the Human Be-In, which featured performances by the Grateful Dead and Jefferson Airplane and was a prelude to the Summer of Love. On August 9, 1995, 20,000 people gathered on the Polo Field for an eight-hour memorial for the Grateful Dead's Jerry Garcia, a hometown hero.

Today the Polo Field is used for the main stage of Outside Lands, where legends like Stevie Wonder, Elton John, Paul McCartney, and The Who have played for massive crowds (more on p. 103). The upper dirt track, which was once for horses, is now for joggers and walkers. The lower paved track continues as a velodrome for bicyclists.

The charming Anglers Lodge is one of the WPA projects in the park. Peek inside if it's open. *(Photo by Jim Watkins)*

Polo Field (see sidebar) and on your right is a small, fenced corral. Depending on the time of day, you may see cyclists doing laps around the paved velodrome track (more on p. 112).

Eventually, the path will go slightly downhill. After passing the restrooms on your right, take the paved road straight ahead up a short, steep climb to the **police horse stables,** built in the 1930s. Follow the road to the right around the stables. The very last building and paddock are still occupied by the park's small team of police horses. The city has had a mounted police force since 1874. Note the green antique drinking fountain for horses across the path from the stable doors!

After the stables, continue on the paved road and take the right fork. A small parking lot will be on your right at 1 mile. Turn left up the stairs to the cottage-like **Anglers Lodge**, built in 1938 as a federal Works Progress Administration project to provide jobs during the Great Depression. Walk right around the building, then down the stairs to reach the casting pools. Turn right alongside the pools. (Don't bother to look for fish—there are none.) A few steps after the first corner, you'll find the signpost for the "Middle Lake Cascade" trail. Follow the winding trail down to **Middle Lake**. Turn left along the lakeshore to follow the Middle Lake Loop Trail, then right at the first junction. Soon you will see a parking lot at 1.5 miles. Bear left to exit the lakeside path, then turn left to walk along the left side of the parking lot.

Turn left on the paved path (watch for bikes!). On your left will be **Hellman Hollow** (formerly Old Speedway Meadow), a remnant of the short-lived "Speedway" built in the 1890s for racing fast horses and horse-drawn carriages, now a picnic area. Eventually, the path will go up a steep slope and reach a parking lot. Walk straight across the parking lot to pick up the path again (next to the parcourse "welcome" sign). Turn right at the restroom building. Take the crosswalk across Middle Drive West to the paved path.

When you reach the drinking fountain, at 2 miles, turn left to follow the sidewalk along MLK Drive. Cross Metson Road and then head straight on the dirt path into the woods. This unpaved route appeared on the 1903 map as a "Bikeway" and was one of several major bike paths created after the bicycling boom of the 1890s. It's still used by cyclists today. Stay on the wide dirt path, take a right at the first fork, then go straight through the next intersection. Continue for about half a mile on the widest dirt trail, bypassing any smaller side trails and never taking any sharp turns. Eventually, you will reach the wide, paved Middle Drive West. Cross the drive, turn to the right, and then take the left road uphill (Overlook Drive).

Turn left on the sidewalk on Transverse Drive. Cross JFK Drive and continue straight along Transverse Drive. Turn right at the well-marked midblock pedestrian crossing. Cross both crosswalks carefully. You are on the same trail you followed at the start of the walk. Stay on the paved path to the end of the walk at the bus stop on Fulton Street.

8 Chain of Lakes

Come for the lakes—stay for the enchanted forests!	
	START AND END POINT: 43rd Avenue and Fulton Street
	DISTANCE: 2 miles roundtrip
	TIME: 1 hour minimum
	ACCESSIBILITY: Paved and dirt trails with some moderate grades up and down on dirt paths
	AMENITIES: A small building with restrooms can be found on JFK Drive, 500 feet west of Chain of Lakes Drive East.

The complete redo of Middle Lake in 2024 has turned this into a hotspot for locals and biodiversity. Be sure to walk along the 800-foot cascading creek. *(Photo by Jim Watkins)*

THE PARK HAS ten lakes, and this walk explores the three that make up the Chain of Lakes, all designed by John McLaren to feel as natural as possible, and built on existing freshwater ponds. The three lakes are each very different and offer their own charms, with Middle Lake now a popular destination after a major renovation. Take time for moments of awe (and aww!) as you look at the waterfalls and wildlife.

GETTING THERE

PUBLIC TRANSIT: The 5 and 5R Muni buses stop right at this hike's starting point at Fulton Street and 43rd Avenue. The 31 and 18 Muni buses have stops within a 10-minute walk.

BICYCLE: Bike racks are by the entrance to the car-free Chain of Lakes Drive West.

DRIVING: There is a small parking area at the start of the route in the park and street parking on JFK Drive.

GET MOVING

Enter the park at 43rd Avenue and Fulton Street and head slightly right toward **North Lake**, then take the path that follows the shore of the lake right (counterclockwise). Note that North Lake is a bird-watching hotspot (more on p. 138). Also, heed the

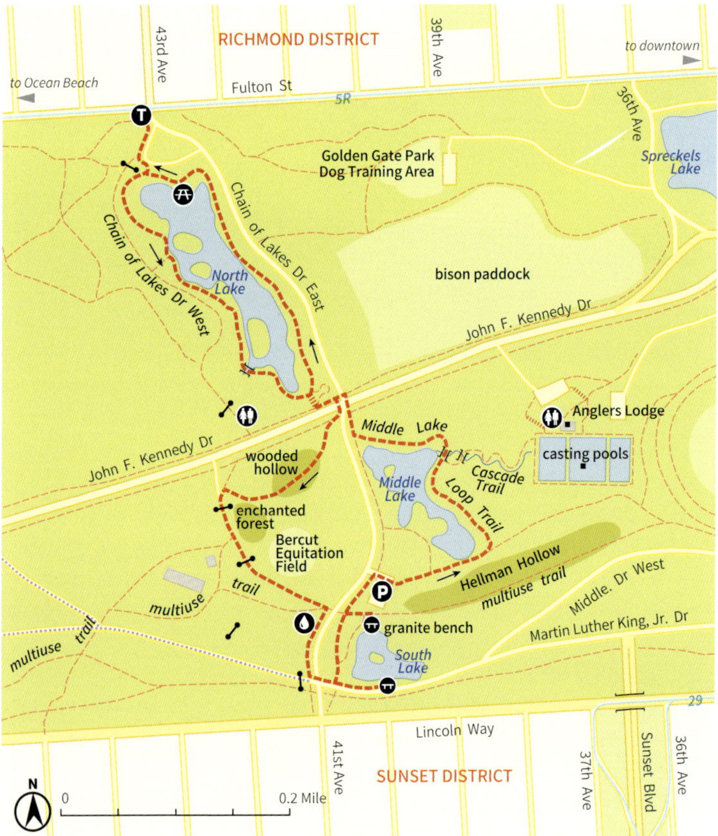

warnings about raccoons and do not feed any wildlife. Continue on the path with the lake on your left until you reach the stairs at the far end of North Lake. Take the stairs up to JFK Drive, or if you prefer, look for the ramp just past the stairs. Turn left. (Note: Restrooms are about five hundred feet to your right.)

At the intersection, cross to the other side of JFK Drive. Turn right and then take the first left into the woods at 0.4 mile. Follow the wide main path as it veers right and then heads straight through the wooded hollow and up the opposite slope. Stay on the wide path as it veers left at the fork. Turn left on the paved path at 0.6 mile. Look to your left to see the enchanting trails curving through the forest created by park gardeners. Optional: Explore the side paths in this area.

When you reach Chain of Lakes Drive West, you'll be at a water fountain. Turn right on the sidewalk and continue a block to Martin Luther King Jr. Drive. Cross Chain of Lakes Drive West and continue straight on the sidewalk to the benches over looking **South Lake**. After enjoying a short rest, backtrack a short distance and turn right on the sidewalk to continue around South Lake. When you reach the multiuse trail, turn right and walk about 40 feet to look at South Lake from this side; you'll see a large granite bench facing the lake.

If the bench looks a bit out of place, it is! Originally placed in Union Square, it was moved here in the 1940s. The bench memorializes two trailblazing women who were also life partners, Fidelia Jewett and Lillien Martin. Jewett was a scientist, teacher, and philanthropist; Martin was a groundbreaking psychologist.

Return to the sidewalk along Chain of Lakes Drive East and walk to the other side of the parking lot to the signs marking the disabled parking spaces. Between them is the entrance to the Middle Lake Loop trail. Follow the path counterclockwise around **Middle Lake**. Optional: About a quarter of a mile around the lake, at the little bridge, turn right to explore the Cascade Trail that runs along the 800-foot meandering creek and waterfalls, and then return to the Middle Lake Loop Trail.

Middle Lake underwent a major overhaul in 2024 that turned this part of the park into a destination, especially for people living in the Avenues. More than 10,000 native plants were planted to provide habitat and food for birds, insects, reptiles, and amphibians, including the protected California red-legged frog. Around you are more than fifty species of flowering shrubs, perennials, ferns, and aquatic plants, including toyon, coastal strawberry, sage, lupine, coyote bush, and rushes.

The path exits onto Chain of Lakes Drive East. Turn right on the sidewalk, and continue to the same intersection with JFK Drive you crossed earlier. Cross the street back to the path around North Lake, reaching it via the stairs or ramp. But this time, take the path to the right to walk on the eastern side of North Lake (counterclockwise) to return to where you started.

9 Hidden in Plain Sight: The Northwest Corner

Take this loop to find an area that most parkgoers miss, especially if you're already going to the Dutch Windmill or want to hike near the Pacific Ocean.	**START AND END POINT:** 43rd Avenue and Fulton Street entrance to Golden Gate Park
	DISTANCE: 1.5 miles roundtrip
	TIME: 1 hour
	ACCESSIBILITY: Rolling terrain, with a variety of paved and dirt surfaces
	AMENITIES: Restrooms are at Chain of Lakes Drive West at JFK Drive and at the Golden Gate Park Golf Course Clubhouse.

THE NORTHWESTERN CORNER of the park is relatively under the radar, even for locals, with the exception of the showy Dutch Windmill and Queen Wilhelmina Garden. This mellow walk explores the area, including the archery range and golf course, revealing unexpected views and pockets of the park—all set against the stunning backdrop of the Pacific Ocean.

GETTING THERE

PUBLIC TRANSIT: The 5 and 5R Muni buses stop right at the starting point for this hike at Fulton Street and 43rd Avenue. The 31 and 18 Muni buses have stops within a 10-minute walk.

BICYCLE: Bike racks are available at the entrance gate to Chain of Lakes Drive West.

DRIVING: There is a small parking area at the start of the route, and street parking on JFK Drive.

GET MOVING

As you enter the park from Fulton Street, immediately take the road to the right. This is the start of Chain of Lakes Drive West. Continue through the yellow posts and stay on the paved road. It's hard to imagine that until the 1980s, this was a road for automobiles. You will notice **North Lake** and the trails on your left (you can walk them on the **Chain of Lakes** hike). Pass beneath a grove of large eucalyptus and Monterey cypress trees planted over a hundred years ago to help create a windbreak from the brutal winds coming off the Pacific.

When the road ends at JFK Drive, turn right on the sidewalk, which goes along a pleasant wooded area before turning to the right and climbing uphill. From this elevation you can glimpse the **Golden Gate Park Golf Course** (more on p. 116) on your right, then views of the ocean, the **Beach Chalet Athletic Fields**, and the **Dutch Windmill** through the trees to the left. The sidewalk will end at 47th Avenue.

Turn right on 47th Avenue at the green entrance sign for the golf course, and then turn right again into the parking lot driveway. Cross the parking lot and follow the path uphill to the **Golden Gate Park Golf Course Clubhouse**. The clubhouse and golf course reopened in 2024 after a complete renovation. Behind the clubhouse is the "nicest patio in Golden Gate Park" (per clubhouse staff). Don't be shy: It's open to the public, and the grill inside is one of the few places you can get an original Hot Dog Bills Burgerdog. The clubhouse also has what are probably the nicest restrooms in the park, all of which are all-gender.

The Clubhouse is open to the public. Feel free to grab a coffee or beer, enjoy the patio, and use the park's nicest restrooms. *(Photo by Jim Watkins)*

Walk back down the path you came up on. When you reach the parking lot, immediately cross to the far right of the parking lot and take the path through the white posts, which leads to the **archery range** (learn more on p. 109). Continue along the left side of the archery range. Exit to 47th Avenue, turn right, and then take the wide dirt path on your right just before Fulton Street. As you head uphill, stay on the wider main dirt path. Optional: Make a detour here to mosey around the trails in this area.

Eventually, all the trails will bring you back to Chain of Lakes Drive West. When you return to Chain of Lakes Drive West, turn left at the yellow posts to get back to the start point.

10 The Northern Edge

From original oak woodlands to views of the Golden Gate Bridge, hike across the entire park to the Pacific Ocean.	
	START POINT: McLaren Lodge, 501 Stanyan Street
	END POINT: Beach Chalet, 1000 Great Highway
	DISTANCE: 4 miles (one-way)
	TIME: 2 hours
	ACCESSIBILITY: Small hills, occasional stairs; surface can be uneven, with some dirt and sand paths
	AMENITIES: Water and restrooms are near the route next to the Conservatory, behind the bandshell in the Music Concourse, inside the de Young Museum, and at Beach Chalet at the end of the walk.

THIS WALK MOSTLY FOLLOWS paths close to the northern edge of the park, with a few exceptions. Locals will discover parts of the park they've never seen before, tourists will enjoy numerous views of the Golden Gate Bridge and the Pacific Ocean, and

The main trail through the coast live oak woodlands is the Phil Arnold Trail, which was dedicated in 2019 to a true hero of the park.

everyone will enjoy the range of forested trails winding through coastal redwoods and old-growth coast live oaks.

You can combine this walk with the **Southern Edge** hike to do a full 8.5-mile perimeter hike of the park. Want a shorter walk? End your hike at any time and catch the 5 or 5R Muni bus, which stop frequently along the entire route. Feeling hungry? You are not far from several Richmond District lunch spots, cafés, and bakeries.

GETTING THERE

PUBLIC TRANSIT: The 5, 5R, 6, 7, and 33 Muni buses all have stops within a few blocks of McLaren Lodge, with the 33 offering the closest stop (just one block). The N Judah streetcar has a stop—Carl and Cole—half a mile away. McLaren Lodge is a stop on the Golden Gate Park Shuttle route, so if you're already in the park, this is a good way to get to the lodge (see sfrecpark.org for current hours of service).
BICYCLE: There are bike racks in front of McLaren Lodge. There are also bikeshare stations near McLaren Lodge at Pompei Circle and JFK Promenade.
DRIVING: There is a curbside drop-off zone in front of McLaren Lodge and an extremely limited amount of free public parking. The closest parking otherwise is street parking on Fulton Street or nearby streets, or the Kezar parking lot on Stanyan Street. There are several free, two-hour ADA spots in front of McLaren Lodge and in a nearby parking zone. On evenings, weekends, and holidays, a limited amount of public parking can be found in the lot behind the lodge.

GET MOVING

Start at **McLaren Lodge**. Coming down the stairs from the lodge, facing **Uncle John's Tree** (more on p. 150), turn right on the asphalt; proceed straight, stay right onto the wide paved path, then take a right at the first Y to head toward the back side of the building. There you'll find a lovely garden between the old building and the newer addition. Notice the charming **Nunan Fountain** from 1933, which was originally for horses and dogs to drink from.

Continue on the path, staying to the left of the parking lot. Turn left at the next fork. At the next intersection, take the **Phil Arnold Trail**, labeled with a large carved stone. Follow the wooden fence along the trail and take the first right at the end of the fence to head up the steps into the **coast live oak woodlands**, a designated old-growth forest of coast live oaks. This is one of the rare parts of the park that was left untouched when it was developed, and it is the same now as it was before San Francisco was established (more on p. 148).

Continue past the circle at the top of the hill (0.3 mile) and walk downhill, then take a right at the sign pointing to Stanyan and Fulton Streets. This will take you to the northeast corner of the park, named **Kathleen's Corner** for volunteer Kathleen Russell, who tended the garden at this entrance to the park for forty years. From here, follow the trail as it makes a sharp left on the flat, paved path. Just before the trail reaches the road (Conservatory Drive East), turn right on the trail marked with a brown signpost. You'll soon have a view across the Richmond District to the Golden Gate Bridge, the Marin Headlands, and the Pacific Ocean.

The trail will reach the intersection of Arguello Boulevard and Conservatory Drive. Continue straight to cross Arguello Boulevard. Take the trail down the wooden steps into the oak trees. Stay on the trail as it winds through a shady valley. You will see an open gazebo

Beach Chalet

There's no need to dine here to check out the murals, exhibits, and restrooms inside; Beach Chalet is open to the public. *(Photo by Jim Watkins)*

Beach Chalet is where you can enjoy the park's most upscale food, with views of the Pacific. Downstairs is the more casual Park Chalet, which has an outdoor patio. Whether or not you're hungry, you should check out this historical building from 1925, which is open to the public (and has public restrooms). The first floor features murals by local artist Lucien Labaudt, painted in 1936 and 1937 with scenes from the park and city at the time. Make sure to look for a depiction of John McLaren sitting on a bench, and don't miss the quotes from local writers like trailblazing San Franciscan Ina Coolbrith, California's first poet laureate. Kids will also love finding the carved mermaids on the stairway.

This building was used during World War II to house members of the US Army, as San Francisco was considered a possible target for enemy attacks. During the Cold War, the US Army used the nearby Beach Chalet Athletic Fields for four defensive weapons, which were hidden behind a fence and trees.

ahead with tables at 0.8 mile, the **Ghirardelli Card Shelter**. Yes, it *was* named for someone in the chocolate company's family, and it was built specifically as a hangout for playing cards. This structure is all that remains of what was once an ornate, glassed-in building.

Continue along the winding dirt path with the shelter on your left, and then turn right on the next paved path to continue along the edge of the park. Continue through the 6th Avenue entrance to the park, with **Skatin' Place** on your left. Jog slightly left to continue along the gravel path that parallels Fulton Street. Soon you will pass a favorite site for rail historians: the old **Powell Street Railroad Station** at 7th Avenue. It was a station for steam trains from 1888 to 1906 and then for cable cars bringing park visitors from downtown, which was considered a great distance at the time. You are now a mile from your start point at McLaren Lodge.

Continue to 8th Avenue and JFK Promenade, cross 8th Avenue, and then turn right on the sidewalk toward the park entrance guarded by bronze animals atop the pillars. Reaching the pillars, turn left onto the paved path to continue along the edge of the park. Pass through the descriptively named **Blue Playground**, with the historical pedestrian tunnel on your left. After the play structure, take the left path uphill.

At JFK Promenade, turn right. The de Young Museum tower will be on your left. Turn right onto the wide dirt path into the **Heroes Grove** redwoods. Follow the wide trail through the redwoods, past the large stone of the World War I monument on your left, then stay right as you head downhill. Keep the ravine on your right and follow the path as it continues downhill and then curves uphill to the right (don't go to the bottom of the ravine). Once you arrive at street level, the **Rose Garden** will be on your left.

Turn right and follow the paved path to the stoplight at Fulton Street. Use the crosswalk to cross Park Presidio Boulevard to continue into **"Lost Golden Gate Park"**: a triangular section of the park that was cut off from the rest in the 1940s by the construction of Crossover Drive and Park Presidio Bypass Drive. This "lost" part of the park is truly off the beaten path, yet has some of the best views of the ocean, Marin Headlands, and Golden Gate Bridge.

You'll notice a couple of mysterious stone rings along the path, built to protect long-gone trees. Water supply to this section was cut off when the highway was constructed, so this landscape has a rougher, unkempt look. The path exits onto busy Crossover Drive. You're now 2 miles from your start point.

The Powell Street Railroad Station was the end of the line for a steam train from downtown to the park.

Take the crosswalk across Crossover Drive and Transverse Drive, being mindful of traffic, and then take a sharp right on the dirt path along Transverse Drive. Just before Fulton Street, turn left on the paved path. On your left is the **disc golf course** (watch for flying discs) and on your right is Fulton Street. The path will soon become unpaved and continues parallel to Fulton Street.

Cross 30th Avenue and continue on the dirt trail to **Spreckels Lake**. At the lake, curve to the right to follow Spreckels Lake Drive, with the lake on your left. Cross 36th Avenue and walk down the steep, sandy path. You are now 3 miles from your start point. The next building on your right is the **Golden Gate Park Senior Center**. When the path reaches the road, turn right and walk on the paved roadway to the **Golden Gate Park Dog Training Area**.

Take the gravel path to the right of the dog training area. Follow this path as it heads downhill through cypress and eucalyptus trees and then becomes a gravel road. You'll pass a concrete maintenance building on your right. Follow the dirt road to Chain of Lakes Drive and exit through the yellow gateposts.

Cross the road carefully to the three yellow gateposts on the other side. Go downhill, turn right, and take the trail along the northern edge of **North Lake**. As you walk with the lake on your left, you'll soon see on your right a set of five yellow posts blocking the road with "Not a Through Street" signs at 3.4 miles. Cross the grass and turn right after the posts to take the wide, unpaved path up the hill. Follow the path as it curves down to the right to 47th Avenue and Fulton Street.

Cross 47th Avenue and pick up the path on the other side of the street. As you approach a three-pronged fork in the path at 3.7 miles, you will see an old maintenance shed on your right. Take the left fork. You'll see another old maintenance building on your left. Just as you might wonder where in the park you are, the **Dutch Windmill** and **Queen Wilhelmina Garden** will appear suddenly on your right. The windmill was used from 1903 to 1913 to pump water to irrigate the park. (The Queen Wilhelmina Garden came later, in 1962, planted with tulips in honor of the long-reigning monarch of the Netherlands.)

Follow the path to JFK Drive, then turn right on the sidewalk. You will be at the entrance to the Queen Wilhelmina Garden. This is arguably one of the most photogenic spots in the park, no matter the weather! At the Great Highway, turn left to cross JFK Drive and continue on the sidewalk to **Beach Chalet** (see sidebar; be sure to stop in).

There are easy public transit options to get you back to the start of the hike. However, since you made it all the way to the Pacific Ocean on foot, you may want to cross the Great Highway for a seaside moment. Optional: You can turn this hike into an 8.5-mile perimeter hike of the entire park by doing the **Southern Edge** hike back to McLaren Lodge (see below).

GETTING BACK

PUBLIC TRANSIT: The Muni bus 18 stops less than a block from the Beach Chalet. The 5, 5R, and 31 buses are all within 10 minutes. The N streetcar is a flat 15-minute walk from here.

BICYCLE: There are bikeshare stations near Beach Chalet.

11 The Southern Edge

Starting at the Pacific Ocean, wind your way through the wilder west side to many of the eastern end's best spots.

START POINT: Beach Chalet, 1000 Great Highway

END POINT: McLaren Lodge, 501 Stanyan Street

DISTANCE: 4.5 miles one-way (see map on p. 204)

TIME: 2 hours

ACCESSIBILITY: Small hills, occasional stairs; surface can be uneven, with some dirt and sand paths

AMENITIES: Restrooms are along the route at Beach Chalet, Boat Playground at 45th Avenue, Mothers' Meadow Playground at 19th Avenue and MLK Drive, the Koret Children's Quarter, and the Flywheel Coffee kiosk.

THE PARK CAN FEEL REMOVED from the Pacific Ocean (at least until those cold winds hit you). But the dunes on which most of the park was built were the product of the Pacific. William Hammond Hall and John McLaren mostly embraced these

The blades of the Murphy Windmill now only spin once a year, at a Dutch celebration called King's Day in April. *(Photo by Jim Watkins)*

natural hills, inextricably linking the park to the ocean. This hike gives you a fresh perspective on the park's origins and undulations, traversing the southern edge from the lesser-known Murphy Windmill through many quiet forests. As you get closer to the city, you'll come upon many of the most beloved destinations in the park, including the historic Koret Children's Quarter.

GETTING THERE

PUBLIC TRANSIT: The Muni bus 18 stops less than a block from the Beach Chalet. The 5, 5R, and 31 bus routes are all within 10 minutes. The N streetcar is a flat 15-minute walk.

BICYCLE: There are bike racks in front of Beach Chalet. There are also bikeshare stations nearby.

DRIVING: The safest and most convenient drop-off location is the Beach Chalet parking lot. There is parking at the large Ocean Beach parking lot, as well as street parking on JFK Drive in Golden Gate Park. ADA parking is available in the Beach Chalet parking lot.

GET MOVING

Start at **Beach Chalet**. Facing the ocean, cross the parking lot and turn left on the multiuse path. Take the first sharp left through the trees (look for a sign pointing to Murphy Windmill), then turn right on the wide path. You are now walking on the berm of a former streetcar line.

At 0.4 mile, you'll see the **Murphy Windmill** on your left, a full 20 feet taller than the Dutch Windmill and built in 1908 to join the Dutch Windmill in irrigating the park. In 1921, a local woman—and daredevil—named Velma Tilden was tied to one of the blades of Murphy Windmill and rode around twenty-five times! The Murphy Windmill also plays a role in the last five minutes of the 1915 Charlie Chaplin film *A Jitney Elopement*, which you can find easily online; it was the first of many movies shot in the park over the years (more on p. 29).

Follow the flat path until it ends. Take the stairway down to the sidewalk on MLK Drive. Turn right on the sidewalk, then turn left at the crosswalk. Cross MLK Drive and continue straight to head up the wide dirt path into the woods parallel to Lincoln Way.

Watch for bikes (this wide path has been a bicycle route since the late 1890s). For the first 2 miles, you will be on a strip of mostly shaded parkland with Lincoln

Way on your right and MLK Drive on your left. As you walk through the woods, stay right at the forks and keep to the rightmost dirt trail closest to Lincoln Way. The trails can be very sandy, revealing the fact that most of Golden Gate Park was built on dunes. You'll soon pass through the **Boat Playground at 45th Avenue**, which has restrooms. Continue along the path as it emerges from the woods and parallels MLK Drive. Cross **Chain of Lakes Drive**. When you see South Lake across the street, you are 1 mile from the start point. Continue on the dirt path as it follows MLK Drive. You will cross the wide Sunset Boulevard, then a paved path at 30th Avenue.

After you cross 25th Avenue, the dirt trail will continue past a small meadow on the left. As the trail passes 22nd Avenue, you will begin to see several large trees in the Hoover Redwood Grove picnic area on your left. Just past these large redwoods, the unpaved trail will curve to the left and meet a paved trail, which you will follow as it curves up toward Crossover Drive (also known as 19th Avenue and Highway 1), a congested highway that unfortunately bisects the park. As you approach Crossover Drive, turn right toward Lincoln Way to arrive at the large stone towers of the **Breon Gate** entrance. Walk through the pedestrian archway, then turn left to cross busy 19th Avenue in the crosswalk. Reaching the other tower, turn left and walk through its archway, then turn right to follow the sidewalk that curves toward and along a black metal fence.

For the next 0.8 mile, you will be following the fence of the Botanical Garden on your right. Along the way, you'll pass the Botanical Garden North Gate, with the Japanese Tea Garden visible across the street.

Continue until you reach the Main Gate of the Botanical Garden at 3 miles. Directly in front of the Main Gate, take the midblock crosswalk across MLK Drive. Turn right on the sidewalk and follow it to the corner, then take a left to stay on the sidewalk on the left side of the street (which is still MLK Drive). Continue walking, with **Big Rec Ball Field** on your left. At the next intersection, where 7th Avenue comes into the park, cross the street using the farther crosswalk. Go uphill toward Lincoln Way, but before reaching the street, turn left to head up the wooden trail stairs into the trees of this narrow strip of parkland.

Continue on this broad path as it goes uphill and downhill. As you go up, you will see Mount Sutro if it's clear (with Sutro Tower on top), on your right. Continue downhill to the intersection of MLK Drive and Kezar Drive, where this unpaved path ends. Leave the unpaved path and cross MLK Drive toward the black fence and then turn left on the sidewalk. Take the first right and follow the path downhill. Restrooms

While it hardly qualifies as a lake, Alvord Lake is the charming centerpiece of the Haight Street entrance of the park. *(Photo by Jim Watkins)*

will be on your left. Turn right to take one of the paths down to the area between the **carousel** and the stone **Sharon Art Studio** (the small building between is the tasty concession stand California Kahve). Continue through the large **Koret Children's Quarter** playground, dating back to 1888; this was the first public playground in the United States.

When you exit the fenced area of the playground, curve left and then take the first right on the next path, going toward the stone pedestrian tunnel with **Little Rec Field** on your right. Go through the tunnel under the **Alvord Lake Bridge**. This tiny bridge, built in 1889, is the oldest reinforced concrete bridge in the United States, and it was a civil engineering breakthrough at the time (there's even a *99% Invisible* podcast episode about it).

After passing tiny **Alvord Lake**, continue straight up the hill to the plaza at the Haight Street entrance to the park. Follow the arrow on the ground pointing to the Page Street bocce courts to go left, then take the first right fork to follow the paved path parallel to Stanyan Street. On your left, you'll pass the **Flywheel Coffee** kiosk, restrooms, and the **bocce courts**. When the path ends at the intersection of Stanyan Street and Kezar Drive, cross Kezar Drive to end your walk at **McLaren Lodge**.

Acknowledgments

Taking on the entirety of Golden Gate Park for this project, with more than 150 years of history and 1,017 acres, was daunting. But with the help of so many people, the best urban park in the world finally has its own guidebook!

I am deeply grateful to Nancy Botkin, who took on the massive task of creating all the walks and hikes. She was truly the perfect person for this part of the book. Nancy was also a creative and positive thought partner throughout the project. Thank you, Nancy, for nerding out with me many times, enjoying an occasional debate on what was book-worthy, and nurturing my obsession with John McLaren.

Thank you to the Godtland family for providing the ideal (and necessary!) writing retreat multiple times so I could write madly while enjoying the view of Sonoma Mountain.

Thank you to everyone who provided their photography to bring the book to life including: Eddie Bartley, Robert Ho, Liam O'Brien, Emily Rosenberg, and Megan Taylor. An extra big thanks to Jim Watkins, who went above and beyond in providing the majority of shots for the book, and to Greg Gaar for sharing his unbelievable historical photo archive (I wish I could have included so many more).

Speaking of history, this guidebook stands on the shoulders of Christopher Pollock's research and book (which Nancy and I refer to as "the park bible"), *San Francisco's Golden Gate Park: 1,017 Acres of Stories*.

I am also deeply grateful for the Western Neighborhoods Project, which is a treasure trove of park history and helpful historians. Special thanks to Nicole Meldahl, Arnold Woods, Chelsea Sellin, and John Freeman. If you love the park and haven't gone to OutsideLands.org and OpenHistorySF.org to look at historic park photos (including hundreds from Greg Gaar's collection) go to your computer right now and be prepared to emerge hours later. And then join the Western Neighborhoods Project!

Opposite: Huntington Falls was built for the 1894 California Midwinter International Exposition.

Thanks to other local historians who have dug into the park's past, providing nuggets or publishing helpful pieces including: Gary Kamiya; Woody LaBounty; Christina Moretta and Andrea Grimes and the rest of the staff at the San Francisco Public Library History Center; David Gallagher; LisaRuth Elliott and Shaping San Francisco / FoundSF; and Peter Hartlaub.

Speaking of Peter Hartlaub, it's Peter, Heather Knight, and Dave Eggers who got me off the fence with deciding to write this book (they don't know this!). I was listening to the Total SF podcast where the three of them gush about the park, and when they deemed it the best urban park in the world, that was it.

Thanks to Gus D'Angelo and Emma Bland Smith for your direct and indirect roles in connecting me with Mountaineers Books, the ideal home for this book. Everyone at Mountaineers Books was so committed to making it great: Kate Rogers, Laura Shauger, Janet Kimball, Sarah Currin, and Melissa McFeeters. And what a delight to have Ben Pease, who knows the park so well, as the cartographer! Dream team.

Many people and organizations provided information and insights that added so much to the book. My thanks to: Lauren Esposito, PhD, with the California Academy of Sciences; the staff at the de Young Museum, especially John Burket; the San Francisco Recreation and Parks Department, especially Phil Ginsburg, Kat Anderson, Shauna Bogetz, and Tamara Aperton; Peter Brastow; Bob Armstrong with the Artists Guild of San Francisco; Liam O'Brien; Gail McGowan and SF CityGuides; volunteers at the SF Botanical Garden; Brandy Kuhl at the Helen Crocker Russell Library of Horticulture at the San Francisco Botanical Garden; Megan Taylor; Andy Chan and Malinda Walker; Whitney Grover with Golden Gate Bird Alliance; the San Francisco Zoo; Nancy DeStefanis and SF Nature; Nature in the City; the Association of Ramaytush Ohlone; Michael Sullivan and SFtrees.com; Jon Toby with the San Francisco Disc Golf Club; Carl Nolte; Nora Gallagher and the San Francisco Lawn Bowling Club; Ann and the Pétanque Club; Zoee Astrachan; the San Francisco Public Library History Center; Miles Epstein; and Steven Pitsenbarger at the Japanese Tea Garden.

Special thanks to Laura Klivans, Nancy Botkin, and Drew Lindsey for reviewing the draft manuscript and adding in your significant park expertise.

To everyone who cares for or builds community in Golden Gate Park: *you* are what makes it the best urban park in the world. This list is endless, but I'd like to give a shout-out to all the park gardeners, whether paid or volunteer; David Miles Jr., Colleen Jones, and the Skatin' Place skaters; Illuminate SF; the people who make fairy doors for the park; Dan Dectis and the Community Music Hangout; the Friday afternoon jazz musicians; and everyone who was part of making JFK Promenade permanent.

To the friends, family members, and fellow writers who encouraged me in writing my first-ever grown-up book (some of whom got dragged on information- or photo-gathering missions): Kirsten and Josh Farrell; Nolan and MJ Anderson; Landon Jones; Andrea Deeken; Jodie Medeiros and Walk San Francisco; the ever-supportive Mom's Night crew; Jenny Fogarty and Zac Ciccala; Meredith Benton; my ever-helpful original critique group members Emma Bland Smith, Meredith Steiner, and Victoria Sanchez; Carol Brownson; Zoe Corbyn and Tom Simonite; Bob and Sally Zielinski; the Lindsey-Thompson-Lambert clan; Thalia Benatatos; and Alexandra Kenin.

And of course, a 1,017-acre size thanks to Drew, Helena, and Elise, for cheering me on and being the biggest part of why I love the park: because of all our time spent and memories made there together.

—Marta Lindsey

I couldn't have done this without the support of the team of enthusiastic and detail-oriented route testers. My deepest gratitude to: Mike Mack of Minneapolis (who tested every route in the book!); Manish Champsee and Jean Doyle; Jean Kao and Magnus Barber; Maria Stokes; Sacha Ortega and Chloe Atreya; Maggie Robbins and Leslie Buck for pointing out the plants along the way; Anna Sojourner; Guy Joaquin; Eric Chase; Andrew Greenberg and Marilyn Adamson; Rich Coffin and Cheryl Brinkman; Dana Weissman and family; Robin Marks; and Juliana Gallin and Fuzzle (RIP).

Also crucial were Lusen Mendel, Marie Jonas, Kelsey Roeder, Alice Lin, and all the other members of the San Francisco Bicycle Coalition's women and non-binary group. At our Friday bike rides through the park, they cheered me on with this project and asked great questions that I then had to research (with many of the answers ending up in these pages).

For so many of the answers, I am grateful to all the dedicated people working in the park, including volunteers. These folks patiently replied to my extremely detailed questions when I was out exploring routes.

Words cannot express the role that my friend LisaRuth Elliott, a historian and writer, played. Also to my husband, Michael "Skibu" Smith, who inspired me by leading a Lakes of Golden Gate Park walk years ago and through his ongoing activism for pedestrian rights and safety in San Francisco.

Although we never met in her lifetime, I am deeply grateful to Bernice Rodgers, arguably the most enthusiastic supervisor of the permits office ever. Researching her started me on the fascinating path deep into the history and secrets of Golden Gate Park, plus led me to her daughter Brenda, who so warmly shared her mother's story with me. You can still meet her in spirit on the car-free road bearing her name in the western end of the park.

—Nancy Botkin

RESOURCES

Books

Aikman, Tom Girvin. *Boss Gardener: The Life and Times of John McLaren*. Lexikos Pub, 1988.

Clary, Raymond H. *The Making of Golden Gate Park: The Early Years: 1865–1906*. Don't Call It Frisco Press, 1984.

Clary, Raymond H. *The Making of Golden Gate Park: The Growing Years: 1906–1950*. Don't Call It Frisco Press, 1987.

McClintock, Elizabeth. *The Trees of Golden Gate Park and San Francisco*. Heyday, 2001.

O'Brien, Liam. *Butterflies of the Bay Area and (Slightly) Beyond*. Heyday, 2025.

Pollock, Christopher. *San Francisco's Golden Gate Park: A Thousand and Seventeen Acres of Stories*. 150th anniversary edition. Norfolk Press, 2020.

Sloan, Doris. *Geology of the San Francisco Bay Region*. University of California Press, 2006.

Sullivan, Mike. *The Trees of San Francisco*. Pomegranate, 2004.

Libraries

San Francisco History Center, San Francisco Public Library
sfpl.org/locations/main-library/sf-history-center

The Helen Crocker Russell Library of Horticulture at the San Francisco Botanical Garden
gggp.org/learn/library-collection

Online Archives and Media

FoundSF.org: This digital history archive is focused on stories, photos, and videos about San Francisco.

Oldmapsonline.org: This site features historical maps of Golden Gate Park over time.

1,017 Acres: Life in the Park: a Substack about Golden Gate Park by writer Susan Freinkel

The Online Archive of California: Visit oac.cdlib.org for descriptions of collections of more than 350 institutions, including libraries, special collections, archives, historical societies, public universities, and museums throughout California.

The *San Francisco Chronicle* and *San Francisco Examiner* Archives: These archives are available through the San Francisco Public Library's digitized historical newspapers at sfpl.org.

The San Francisco Historical Photograph Collection: Visit digitalsf.org to search through more than 50,000 historical photographs of the San Franciso area, public records, and more.

The Western Neighborhoods Project: Visit outsidelands.org for history articles, podcasts, and an extensive historic photo archive.

Index

G

H

I

J

K

L

M

N

O

P

Q

R

S

Marta Lindsey (Photo by Emily Rosenberg)

About the Authors

MARTA LINDSEY has lived just a block from Golden Gate Park for almost twenty years. Lindsey has explored every corner of the park on foot and bicycle, most often with her family.

Her award-winning picture book, *Golden Gate Park: An A to Z Adventure*, introduces readers to many of the park's unique features and surprising stories. In *Discovering Golden Gate Park: A Local's Guide*, Lindsey takes her curiosity for the park to the next level to connect visitors with a wide range of experiences and perspectives, covering every aspect of her beloved backyard.

When in the park, she always keeps an eye out for herons, hawks, and her friends.

NANCY BOTKIN started mapping her world when she was seven years old alongside her grandfather, a surveyor, and went on to study geography in college. Botkin has been designing and leading walking and biking tours in San Francisco for more than two decades. She also teaches classes in the forgotten art of map folding.

Botkin lives near the park's Panhandle and visits the park nearly every day.

MOUNTAINEERS BOOKS

SKIPSTONE BRAIDED RIVER

recreation • lifestyle • conservation

MOUNTAINEERS BOOKS, including its two imprints, Skipstone and Braided River, is a leading publisher of quality outdoor recreation, sustainability, and conservation titles. As a 501(c)(3) nonprofit, we are committed to supporting the environmental and educational goals of our organization by providing expert information on human-powered adventure, sustainable practices at home and on the trail, and preservation of wilderness.

Our publications are made possible through the generosity of donors, and through sales of more than 700 titles on outdoor recreation, sustainable lifestyle, and conservation. To donate, purchase books, or learn more, visit us online:

MOUNTAINEERS BOOKS

1001 SW Klickitat Way, Suite 201 • Seattle, WA 98134

800-553-4453 • mbooks@mountaineersbooks.org • www.mountaineersbooks.org

An independent nonprofit publisher since 1960

LEAVE NO TRACE Mountaineers Books is proud to support the Leave No Trace Center for Outdoor Ethics, whose mission is to use the power of science, education, and stewardship to ensure a sustainable future for the outdoors and the planet. The Leave No Trace program is focused specifically on human-powered (nonmotorized) recreation. For more information, visit www.lnt.org.

YOU MAY ALSO LIKE:

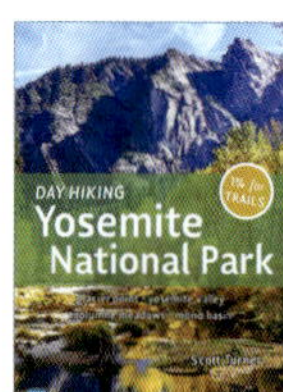